MAKING WEBSITES WIN

Making
Websites
Win

Apply the customer-centric
methodology that has doubled
the sales of many leading websites

Dr Karl Blanks & Ben Jesson
Founders of Conversion Rate Experts

Foreword by Avinash Kaushik
Digital Marketing Evangelist, Google

Conversion Rate Experts

The clients of Conversion Rate Experts (CRE) all bring unique circumstances, aims, market positioning, web presence, expertise, and opportunities to the table. The client stories and testimonials presented in this book therefore cannot be viewed as "typical" results because each client came to CRE with a unique situation and each was provided with unique solutions or recommendations. Each should be viewed and interpreted as a unique case study—some with more detail than others, but each presenting insight into that company's specialized experience with CRE.

MAKING WEBSITES WIN

Apply the customer-centric methodology that has doubled the sales of many leading websites

ISBN   978-1-5445-0053-9 *Hardcover*
       978-1-5445-0051-5 *Paperback*
       978-1-5445-0052-2 *Ebook*

To our brilliant colleagues in Conversion Rate Experts.

To our equally great clients.

To all our company's friends and followers, who have
helped us in innumerable ways over the past ten years.

And to the friends and families of everyone who works so hard at
Conversion Rate Experts. Thank you for helping to make it all happen.

Contents

About the authors

DR. KARL BLANKS and BEN JESSON help websites win. They are the founders of Conversion Rate Experts (CRE), the world's leading agency for conversion rate optimization (CRO)—a term coined by the company in 2007.

Over the past ten years, CRE has worked in over 80 different verticals, in 9 languages, and in 22 countries, helping to optimize the profits of some of **the web's most sophisticated companies**, including:

- Many **Silicon Valley giants**—the world's biggest, most successful websites.
- Websites of leading **blue-chip enterprises**.
- Award-winning, fast-growing **startups**.

CRE increases the profits of businesses scientifically by analyzing their websites' visitors, creating optimized pages and then A/B testing them to measure the increase in sales. It has generated billions in revenue for its clients and double- and triple-digit improvements are the norm.

CRE is the recipient of a Queen's Award for Enterprise for Outstanding Achievement in Innovation, the UK's top award for businesses. The award was given for CRE's work codifying the methodology that the world's leading companies now use to improve their websites.

How to get the most value from this book

Links to resources for growing your business

The electronic version of this book contains links to many great resources for growing your business. The paper version doesn't contain any links, because links add clutter and tend to age quickly. Don't despair, though. For nearly everything we've mentioned, assume that we've chosen wording that will allow you to find it easily in a search. Alternatively, you can see all of the links at www.conversion-rate-experts. com/book-links/.

Our podcast

You can hear some of our most popular talks by subscribing to the Conversion Rate Experts podcast. You can find details at www.conversion-rate-experts.com/podcasts/.

Free gifts and goodies

One of the great services we provide is that of a filter, directing our followers to the best new tools, companies and sources of useful information. If you'd like to be kept up to date with our new discoveries, get our free email newsletter from www.conversion-rate-experts.com/gifts/. You'll be in good company—our subscribers include people from many of the world's leading companies.

Plus, when you join, you'll get some useful reports, including examples of winning pages we've designed that have more than doubled the sales of our clients.

The free guides accompanying this book help you get started quickly.

All profits from this book go to **feeding chronically hungry children**

CRE pays for the ongoing feeding of 280 children in Liberia. The program is run by Mary's Meals, a charity that sets up school feeding programs in some of the world's poorest communities, where hunger and poverty prevent children from gaining an education.

All proceeds from this book will be donated to Mary's Meals to help it continue its great work.

Praise from clients who have implemented the advice in this book

We've grown many companies using the techniques described in this book. Below are some quotes, taken from our website, from clients we've helped over the last ten years.

"Really extraordinary 'off-the-chart' results." —**Google**, the leading internet technology company (CRE has worked with Google on several projects, including the launch of Google's Android phone.)

"Conversion rate optimization was my secret weapon for growth at companies like Dropbox, Eventbrite and LogMeIn. After meeting the team at Conversion Rate Experts I learned that I was only scratching the surface of the potential gains from conversion rate optimization. They are by far the most advanced group in conversion rate optimization that I've ever worked with. Their approach is truly the best I've ever seen." —**Sean Ellis, Dropbox**'s first marketer and founder of **GrowthHackers.com.**

"About $10 million of increased potential revenue. Before using Conversion Rate Experts, it was a lot of guessing." —**Jenny Craig**, the leading weight-loss company.

241% increase in sign-ups for MyFitnessPal. "We've seen more than 4X increases in conversion rate on some pages, which we've been thrilled about. I think there isn't a company in the world that couldn't benefit from working with these guys." —**MyFitnessPal**, the world's largest diet-and-fitness community, which went on to sell for half a billion dollars.

"It's been really remarkable to see that process in action...and to realize that this is a process. They have helped Moz add more than $1 million to our bottom line this year. Our conversion rate is up 170% of what it was four months ago. They're the best in the business." —**Rand Fishkin, Moz**, the search marketing industry's leading SEO software provider, with a community of hundreds of thousands members.

"They increased our conversion rate by 300%. What can I say? They've taught us more about our customers in the last six months than I knew about our customers in the last four years. They were fantastic in telling us exactly what to test on the sites to get the best results." —**Vodafone**, one of the world's largest wireless telecoms providers.

"They helped us get our CRO program off the ground. We now have a much deeper understanding of some of the key customer pain points and, more importantly, a well-defined road map on how to address them." —**Hertz**, the car-rental company with locations in 150 countries.

"We've seen about a five-fold increase in our business, and they've been a huge part of making that happen." —**SimpliSafe**, which designs—and markets—home security alarms.

"They were able to take us to territory that we might have felt internally a bit uncomfortable with, and might not have gone there ourselves. They balance strategy and execution with aplomb." —**goHenry**, a financial services technology (FinTech) company that combines web and mobile apps.

"Conversion Rate Experts were looking for monumental wins, and suggested big changes across our business. They recommended, and helped us to build, what became the second-busiest financial community in the UK." —**money.co.uk**, one of the UK's most popular financial comparison websites.

"They passed amazing amounts of knowledge off to our team and inspired our team with their enthusiasm and passion for what they do. We've even had some product test pages where they've converted 100% better than the previous page." —**Cogeco Peer 1 Hosting**, one of the world's top-five hosting providers, hosting more than one percent of the internet.

"We gained confidence about making big changes because CRE told us that it's the big changes that would have the big impact." —**TopCashback**, which we have helped to be the fifth-fastest-growing company in the UK, growing sales by 2,600% (that's 27 times) in three years.

"I learned a tremendous amount. They are the best in the business." —**PayPal**, one of the world's largest internet payment companies.

"Each percentage point of conversion is very, very important to us and worth a lot of money. Great fun, great results, great return on investment." —**888.com**, the high-profile gaming website.

"It was a professional dream come true for me to have worked with them. In some of the places like the top of the funnel, we almost doubled our conversion rates. It's helped all of us on the team get better at what we do." —**TINYpulse**, an online B2B software platform for engaging employees.

"Conversion rate is the fastest, easiest way to see an increase in your business. The conversion rate was originally less than 5%, and Conversion Rate Experts increased it to 20%–25%." —**Voices.com**, a leading recruitment platform for voice-over artists, having a user base of over 200,000 individuals and companies.

363% increase in conversion rate for **Crazy Egg**, the leading click-mapping platform. "Instead of saying, 'We want to do this, or we want to do that, or I think this would be best for the business,' they got data to back up their decisions and they did that. Which is why we had such a substantial lift." —**Neil Patel**, founder. "They focused on understanding our customers. We believe that led to the increase in conversions." —**Hiten Shah**, founder.

63% increase in sales for **Morphsuits,** the fancy dress company that became the UK's 18th fastest growing company. "We know, when we're thinking about making changes, that anything that they're suggesting is backed up by the data." —**Morphsuits**

"If you don't have a solid conversion rate plan, I would definitely advise you to get in touch with Conversion Rate Experts." —**Dell,** the multinational computer technology company.

"Conversion Rate Experts are by far and away the number one in the world. They have helped us transform our business and our processes around testing. As a direct result of working with Conversion Rate Experts, we've doubled our revenue." —**HomeFinder,** a leading real-estate website.

"I went into this project fairly skeptical that we'd be able to achieve a 30%+ improvement. At 50%+, it far exceeded our expectations." —**AAG,** America's largest provider of government-insured reverse mortgages.

"Working with Conversion Rate Experts has been extremely stunning in terms of results. It's definitely driving a lot of revenue." —**Xero,** the disruptive cloud software company.

"The decision making process is based on real data, tested data, rather than just gut feeling. The results that we've achieved have been very impressive." —**Companies Made Simple,** the company formation service that has created over half a million companies.

"The work that we've done with Conversion Rate Experts has resulted in additional revenue of around £1 million per year. It's been a huge learning experience for the entire team. I wish we had done it a lot earlier." —**Health Express,** an online clinic.

"Sales have increased from £16 million to £31 million per year." —**Sunshine.co.uk,** an online travel operator.

"They are brilliant. The results speak for themselves. Sales nearly tripled." —**Broadband.co.uk,** a leading comparison website for broadband services.

"The results have been great." —**FreestyleXtreme,** "Earth's largest action-sports store."

"They show you how to increase your conversion rate in a structured, analytical and scientific manner. On some of our online shop pages, we increased our conversion rate by up to 100%." —**DefShop,** one of Europe's leading online hip-hop clothing retailers.

"We've been really pleased with our experience with Conversion Rate Experts. We've seen uplift in the order of 50%, 60%, even up to 100% for some of the individual tests." —**Dr Dave Chaffey, Smart Insights,** a marketing authority website that helps marketers to plan, manage and optimize their marketing.

"Sales doubled. They've instilled a testing culture within our company." —**PhotoShelter,** a worldwide leader in photography portfolio websites.

"Some of our senior executives didn't understand how CRO could have such a big financial impact. CRE understands our pain, our industry, and our visitors' frustrations. One test alone gave a 44% increase." —**The Foundry,** a visual-effects software company whose clients include Pixar, ILM, Walt Disney Animation Studios, and Sony Pictures Imageworks.

Foreword by Avinash Kaushik, Digital Marketing Evangelist, Google

If you ask "why experiment" to people who live and champion experimentation, they'll answer that it allows decisions to be based on data. This is true.

Or, they may tell you that it allows you to get answers fast, without needing to have long debates with your team. This is also true.

Or, you'll hear that, because one never knows exactly who the visitor is, it is difficult to anticipate the visitors' expectations—and hence why not let an n-variable multivariate experiment figure out the best solution for each type of visitor. This is especially true.

Or, you'll hear a string of explanations around statistics, confidence intervals, and significance—that a business should be improved with the same discipline and control that would be applied to most feats of manufacturing and engineering. I like this; why not overcome all human barriers via brute force math! :-)

The above reasons are certainly exciting and contribute to why I champion experimentation. They are not at the core, though.

I see experimentation as a solution to a set of pernicious problems with business culture. I am heartbroken about the power dynamic in most organizations, where decisions are based not on customer needs but the opinions of the person with the most senior job title. (In a speech in 2006, I framed this as HiPPO-driven decision-making—HiPPO standing for the Highest Paid Person's Opinion.) Experimentation reduces that power dynamic with amazing results.

In addition, I deeply believe in heuristic evaluations, in which a broad cross section of company employees use a website or mobile app as customers. Heuristic evaluations create a democracy of ideas, capturing insights from beyond the User Experience team and Digital team. The only way to allow this democracy to thrive is to build an experimentation model—to put all the ideas through testing.

In my experience, most companies operate as if the world is static. As if tastes don't change, preferences don't evolve, and disruptive competitors don't show up. In reality, *change is the only constant*. Experimentation assumes this is true and fosters a culture of mental agility that constantly explores boundaries (and pushes against them).

Finally, most people and companies are risk-averse. What I love the most about experimentation is that it allows us to accommodate for the short-term risk we are willing to tolerate. You may be deeply shy, your company may be a cash cow, and even the slightest change to the ecosystem may mean death, but that's no problem. Experimentation allows you to dial-in the level of risk you want to take (you may even choose to show a test to only a small fraction of your visitors). On the other hand, if you realize that taking bold risks is the only way to protect your confident position in the market, then experimentation allows you to execute precisely that—to learn and keep kicking butt!

It's about leveraging experimentation to influence a shift in culture, as we all know *culture eats strategy for breakfast.*

That is the reason you should buy this lovingly crafted book. The deep and broad digital experience Karl and Ben have accumulated in their years of practice is reflected in every chapter.

The book is broken into easily digestible chunks. Section One is best shared with every boss who stands in your way. Section Two will help you quickly set up the foundations on which your ideas democracy can flower. Section Three will give you a lifetime of ideas that will fuel the fundamental shift you are trying to accomplish.

If you are standing in a bookstore wondering if you want to buy this book, jump to the section about how "Winning websites...manage complexity" and scan Step 7. Then rush to the cashier to check out.

A culture of experimentation has benefits that far surpass "this button is better than that" or "this offer is better than that."

Solve for culture and your career will never be the same again.

Carpe diem!

AVINASH KAUSHIK

DIGITAL MARKETING EVANGELIST, GOOGLE

AUTHOR OF *WEB ANALYTICS 2.0* AND
WEB ANALYTICS: AN HOUR A DAY

Why most web design is done wrong

—and how to do it right,
like the winners

Why this is **the only book of its kind** (and why it will transform your website, your business and your career, like it has ours)

Most websites lose. Almost all of them.

Many of them never make a profit. Like chocolate teapots, they look nice but flop as soon as you pour hot customers into them.

Others are successful at first, and then get pushed out of business by their competitors.

This book is about how to buck the trend, to make websites that customers love and that are outrageously profitable.

It has the ability to transform your business and your career. Really. That's an extraordinary claim—and extraordinary claims require extraordinary proof.

So here goes:

1. This book is based on experimentally proven facts—not theory

Have you ever looked at a company's marketing materials and wondered, "Does this really make people buy?"

We have. And in 2005, we began a quest to find out for certain.

One of us, Ben, was running the website for a company that sold phones for travelers. The other, Karl, was a Cambridge PhD scientist. Together, we discussed how we'd be able to carry out scientific experiments on the website.

We'd change a page and then measure—via an A/B

test—whether our new version had increased (or decreased) the company's sales.

The results were astonishing. Within a year, we managed to triple—to $9 million—the sales of the company—even though the worldwide demand for travel phones was decreasing by 15% per year:

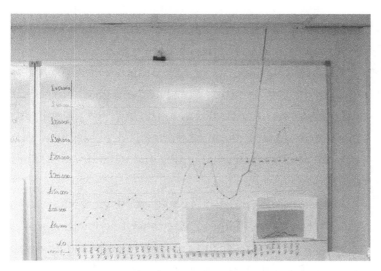

Sales went through the roof the first time we applied A/B testing to a company. Rather than rescaling the axes, we drew on the wall, hoping to penetrate the ceiling tiles. (Those dashed lines represent interim forecasts we kept beating.)

In doing so, we began to build a database of what works (and what doesn't).

Since then, we have applied the same methodology to hundreds of companies. Double- and triple-digit improvements have been the norm, and many of the companies have won awards for fast growth. With each success (and failure), we update our database of what works. And each time an activity turns out to be fruitful (or fruitless), we adjust our methodology accordingly.

In this book, we have distilled many of the most successful ones—the activities and strategies that most reliably grow a business.

It's exciting to have the power to walk into any business and be able to permanently, dramatically, and measurably grow its sales—all without having to leave the building. Most salespeople dream of being able to do that.

You see, the majority of web design and copywriting is still in the pre-scientific age. The average webpage was designed less scientifically than the average toilet brush. Most web designers rely on inspiration, not experimentation. They are oblivious to what works and what doesn't. They violate proven principles.

By the time you finish this book, you'll know what works in web design. You'll know how to write copy that works. And you'll be able to easily spot the mistakes in any webpage—or, indeed, in any marketing materials.

2. The techniques in this book are teachable

On the strength of our success with the travel phone company, we published an article about the approach we had developed. It immediately went viral. On that week, according to the statistics service Alexa.com, our website was the third fastest growing in the world.

The following day, we received an email out of the blue from one of Google's senior managers, who invited us to become the first worldwide consulting partner for Google's testing tool.

And so our company, Conversion Rate Experts, was born.

At the time, hardly anyone was doing this type of marketing. (We even gave it a name: conversion rate optimization, or CRO.)

As we grew, we hired new team members. We discovered that the most successful ones were readers of our blog. So we continued to publish valuable articles with the ulterior motive that each one attracted both clients and new team members.

Plus, every time we published an article, we received emails from people telling us how it had helped them to grow their businesses.

This book is a compilation of the most useful of those articles. For the first time, they are organized in an order that allows you to quickly become great at conversion. Importantly, the book teaches you the right *mental models*, so your understanding of conversion will be deep and intuitive.

Of course, there's a limit to what a book can achieve. A book about songwriting won't turn you into Paul McCartney, and a book about CRO—even a dense one like this—won't make you great at conversion overnight. However, it does contain ample information to generate millions for a company.

The best conversion practitioners are like sponges, obsessed with learning. (Which, come to think of it, sponges aren't. Who came up with that analogy?)

3. This book works whatever your situation

This book is about universal truths. We have yet to find a business for which the techniques in this book don't apply. We have applied our methodology to pretty much all kinds of websites:

- **In nine languages**
- **In twenty-two countries worldwide:** Australia, Canada, China, Denmark, Finland, France, Germany, India, Ireland, Israel, Italy, Japan, Lithuania, Malaysia, New Zealand, Norway, Serbia, Spain, Sweden, United Arab Emirates, United Kingdom, and United States
- **Of all sizes**—from startups to large enterprises
- **In business-to-consumer (B2C) and business-to-business (B2B)**
- **In more than eighty industry verticals**, including finance, health, retail, travel, technology, leisure, and food (you name it, we've sold it)
- **With different types of product:** selling physical goods, services, software, and information
- **With all types of business:** merchants, affiliates, publishers, social networks, e-commerce and lead-generation sites
- **In many media and formats:** desktop websites, mobile websites, native mobile apps, email marketing, offline advertising, and more

The book is useful for whatever job role you have:

- If you are **creating your first website**, and you are hoping that it will drive results (rather than just be a brochure website), then this book will help you to understand what the pages need to say—which is much more important than *how* the pages are created.
- If you are a **web designer or marketing executive**, this book will give you key skills and resources to make websites that beat their competitors and dominate their market.
- If you are a **CEO or in senior management**, this book will reveal the key activities on which your team should be concentrating.

In short, the skills you learn from this book will work for you now, and for whatever you do next.

4. What you will—and won't—get from this book (this book focuses on improving websites—because that's what the most successful web businesses do)

In the 1990s, websites were designed for designers, whose goals were typically (1) to use the project as an opportunity to learn the technologies (Flash, XML, CSS, and others) and (2) to populate their portfolios to show off their newfound capabilities. It wasn't uncommon for a website to be impossibly difficult to use.

In 2000, websites were designed for search engines. To get traffic from search engines, webmasters obsessed over search engine optimization (SEO), making websites "search engine friendly." Unfortunately, the search engines, which were still primitive, accidentally rewarded some practices that were very user-unfriendly, including pages that were stuffed with keywords to the point of being illegible, light gray text on a white background, and "links pages" with endless reciprocal links.

In 2010, websites were designed for companies. Search engines had become less trickable, and so agencies became free to focus on what their clients wanted. And what did the clients want? Well, some of them wanted quirky diagonal navigation bars, some wanted parallax scrolling, and some wanted spinny icons. Others wanted best practices, crammed with marketing techniques and things "borrowed" from competitors. They wanted the kind of thing you see when you browse galleries of website themes.

And that's where we are today.

However, throughout that period, there were a small number of companies that didn't follow those trends. These companies, **the most successful websites, focus on their customers.** Customer-centric design was—and still is—surprisingly rare. The websites look nothing like the ones you see in theme galleries. Customers like them, they visit them often, and they spend a lot. Customer-centric, customer-optimized websites are winning. They are the subject of this book.

If you study any one of the winning websites, you'll find they are built of "engines" of conversion, of perfected landing pages and irresistible offers, of compelling copy and user-friendly interfaces, of viral loops and streamlined order flows. And if you visit the companies themselves, you'll find that their team members are engineers finely tuning those conversion engines.

Web companies that are struggling, on the other hand, tend to focus on different things. Some of them spend their time on brute-force SEO. Others prioritize pretty web design. Many don't ever change their websites, because they have created knots of complexity that they *can't* change. Of course, those disciplines, and many others, are important. But we find that they become easy when you have created a high-converting website.

So, important as they are, this book will not address many aspects of web design and marketing. You'll need a different book if you want to learn HTML, CSS, JavaScript, SEO, or advertising. In this book, we encourage you to focus on what's essential: Creating pages that visitors love and that convert like crazy. If coding is an obstacle for you, you can get great results using this book's methodology with a website builder tool like SquareSpace, Wix, Shopify, Big-Commerce (a former client of ours), LeadPages, Unbounce, ClickFunnels, or PageWiz. Then, imagine how easy it is to get visitors once you have created a website that people love and that has a huge lifetime customer value. Advertising becomes simple when you can afford to outbid all the competition. SEO is a piece of cake when you have a website that people *want* to link to.

5. This book works even on the most sophisticated companies

Our clients include many of the world's most sophisticated web companies. In fact, we believe we have designed pages for more top 500 websites than any other company. This has been both a privilege and a curse. We have been fortunate enough to work with some of the world's best marketers, and we have had to improve upon some of the world's most difficult-to-beat pages.

As such, our methodology has had a trial by fire.

We once read an article called something like "100 must-have web analytics reports." Anyone who's familiar with the Pareto principle will know that there aren't 100 must-have anythings. At the end of a project, we ask ourselves the following question: "If we had to repeat that project in one-tenth of the time, what were the vital few activities that were most fruitful? What could we do differently next time?"

This book is about the vital few.

6. This book works on all marketing materials, not just websites

Even though this book is about optimizing webpages, it's equally applicable to any content that is important enough to be hyperoptimized.

The techniques can be applied with great success to almost any media, provided it's important enough to be worth making great. We've used it successfully on press releases, marketing email sequences, video scripts, webinars, print ads, Facebook ads, and much more.

Terminology and other details

Throughout this book, for brevity, we will usually refer to "products" when we mean "products and services." All of the advice is just as applicable to services. (And we should know—we sell services.)

We don't get paid for mentioning or recommending any tools or techniques.

We mention the tools and products of several companies that have been clients of ours. In all cases, we were using and recommending these companies before they became clients. (We reference hundreds of resources throughout the book, so it was inevitable that a few of them would be clients.)

Ulterior motives: Why we wrote this book

We wrote this book for two reasons:

Might you be a kindred spirit?

We want this book to be a mechanism for attracting like-minded specialists. Our company mission is to remain the best in the world at CRO—and that's a tall order.

You can imagine that people who are proven experts at website creation, copywriting, analytics, marketing research, design, and so on are in great demand and have no problem being happily employed. If you believe you're world-class at CRO, and you're up for stiff challenges and high rewards, we'd love to hear from you.

If your company isn't yet large enough to be our client...

Many of our clients were small when they first started reading our articles. In fact, we often hear from readers who attribute their success to the advice we published.

This book provides you with enough information to more than double the sales of an early stage business.

And, who knows, perhaps one day we will work together.

What you'll get from each section

If you want to become an expert in CRO, you'll probably want to read all of this book. If, on the other hand, you want to carry out CRO for only one project, you can dip in and out of the relevant chapters.

Here's how this book is structured:

Section 1: The one you're halfway through reading

In the rest of this section ("Why Most Web Design Is Done Wrong—and How to Do It Like the Winners"), we define what conversion entails (when it's done right). We explain why it should be the number-one priority for your company (and for your career)—as it is for the world's most successful web companies. We describe The Power Law of CRO and how it can drive a company into an economic "virtuous circle" of growth. This will help you to win the support and enthusiasm of your colleagues.

We also point out the conversion principles that are followed by the top web companies—the winners—and that are strikingly absent from most other web companies.

Most people do CRO the wrong way round. They behave like physicians prescribing remedies before having diagnosed the patient. These "malpracticing physicians of marketing" prescribe testimonials, guarantees, and punchy headlines—and have no idea why the visitors aren't taking action. We introduce our customer-centric DiPS (Diagnose → Problem → Solution) approach, which thrashes the alternative—as you'd expect, given that the alternative is so absurd.

Section 2: Diagnosis (the D of DiPS)

In Section 2, ("Diagnosis: Understanding Why Your Visitors Aren't Converting"), we take you on a grand tour of tools and techniques you can use to diagnose and improve your website's problems. To overextend the medical analogy, these are the web stethoscopes, landing page thermometers, and the homepage ear-microscope doodads. These techniques will allow you to deeply understand your visitors—and how they interact with your website. That way, you'll empathically understand them, and you'll be able to identify exactly why they aren't converting into customers.

Section 3: Common problems and solutions (the P and S of DiPS)

Fortunately, there aren't an infinite number of reasons why visitors don't convert. In fact, our research has revealed that most websites underperform in just fourteen ways. In Section 3, ("Making Websites Win: The Most Common Problems That Make Web Visitors Abandon—And Proven, Easy-To-Implement Solutions") we devote a chapter to each of them. In each chapter, we describe the most effective techniques for getting your website "firing on all fourteen cylinders."

Section 4: Bringing it all together

In Section 4, we describe a case study of how we helped to grow a financial-technology company by 470% in just a year. We reveal exactly how the steps were carried out, so you can see how the principles and techniques described above come together in practice—with record-breaking results.

Okay, that's enough overviewing. It's time to explain what conversion entails (when done right), and why it should be the number-one priority for your company—and for your career.

How we define conversion rate optimization (CRO)
What is a conversion rate?

Your conversion rate is the percentage of your visitors who end up reaching a given goal. This diagram illustrates it:

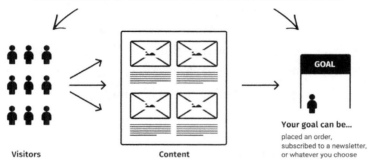

The most useful definition of conversion rate is broad.

Two things are worth noting:

1. **The "content" can be *any* item of messaging or any user interface.** Of course, it can be a landing page, but it can also be a checkout page, an explainer video, the warranty application card that comes with a product, an email asking customers to refer their friends, the sales script that a customer service operator uses, a radio ad, ... you get the idea. We have optimized all of the above and more. If you restrict yourself to landing pages, you're going to struggle to triple a company's sales.

2. **The "goal" is often to maximize sales—but not always.** The goal of an early-stage social network, for example, may be to acquire new non-paying users. The goal of a knowledge base article may be to minimize the number of customers who need to call customer service, so the call center operatives can have less-hurried cigarette breaks. Always, the goal is to optimize the

content for *whatever it was created for*—its *raison d'etre* (that's French for "raisin for eating." Who needs Google Translate?). The content exists to do a job, so it must excel at that job. You may think it's obvious to *optimize something for its entire reason for existing.* Incredibly, in the world of marketing, it's vanishingly rare.

What is A/B testing?

A/B testing is a powerful way to increase conversion rates. Here's how it works:

If you had two possible headlines for your webpage but couldn't decide which one to use, you could run an A/B test in which

- half of your visitors would see Headline A, and
- the other half would see Headline B.

You could then tally the orders for each headline and determine which headline brought you the most.

A/B testing software makes it easy to carry out such tests. Each of your visitors will see a different version of the page—Version A or Version B, or even Version C, D, or E—and then the software will work out, on average, which of the elements performed the best. The winner can then be promoted.

In most tests, Version A is the existing version, often called the "control," which you are trying to beat.

If we were to use A/B testing software on the following page, we could test the following:

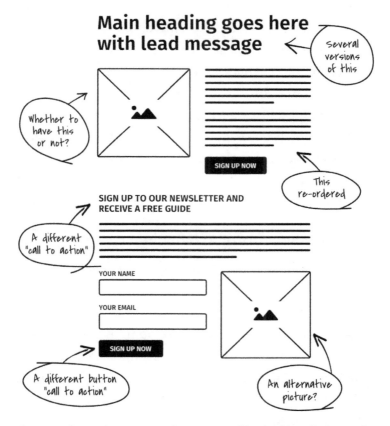

On every webpage, there are many changes you could make to increase your profits.

Powerful, isn't it?

What is multivariate testing?

Most A/B testing software also allows you to carry out *multivariate tests*. What are they?

Multivariate tests let you effectively carry out several A/B tests concurrently, so you make the most of your traffic. So while you are testing which headline to use, you could also test other page elements—such as text, images, prices, offers, and buttons—all at once. Each visitor will see a different combination of headline, text, images, and buttons. Then, once enough data have been collected, the multivariate testing software will tell you which version of each page element, *on average*, brought in the most customers.

Throughout this book, we'll use "A/B testing" as a catch-all term to describe A/B testing, multivariate testing, and any other types of scientifically controlled experiments.

Four huge benefits of A/B testing

When you A/B test, you get the following benefits:

1. You get to discard your missteps

Most marketing is based on mere opinions; A/B testing reveals the truth. If a test doesn't produce a winner, you haven't lost a thing; you learn from it and discard the losing variation. You certainly don't keep it, which is what happens in companies that don't test.

One of our first clients, whose sales we more than tripled, stopped A/B testing after we finished working with it. Its marketing manager then began making radical changes. He persuaded his team that there was no need to A/B test, because the changes were "obviously improvements." Within a year, the company's sales had plummeted, and no one in the company knew why. The marketing manager was fired. Had he A/B tested his changes, he wouldn't have broken the company.

The following story from Microsoft's Senior Statistician, Roger Longbotham, describes how Microsoft avoided a similar disaster:

> We ran an experiment for a site where the management was reluctant to run the test because they considered it a "no-brainer" that the treatment would win. We agreed the value proposition looked quite promising but proceeded with the experiment. The treatment had some unexpected and subtle negative aspects that would not have been detected had we not run the experiment. If the treatment had been launched we estimate the annual loss to the site would have been in the millions of dollars.

2. You keep only your successes

If something works, you get to know. So you never accidentally throw away something that works. This process repeats over and over, meaning that only better-performing versions of pages are kept, so your conversion rate (and revenue) can only go up.

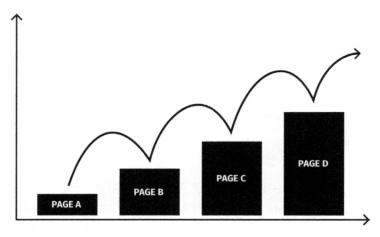

With iterative testing, your profits can only go up—because you keep only the winners.

3. You learn what you should be doing more (and less) of

A/B testing is like a compass: It tells you which direction to move in. One of our clients, a company in the telecoms industry, was debating whether to lower the price of its top-selling phone. The phone was already the lowest priced in the marketplace. To measure how price sensitive the company's visitors were, we A/B tested the existing price against zero dollars (completely free of charge). To everyone's surprise, the zero-dollar offer didn't sell more phones. Our research revealed that users were concerned that the free-phone deal was "too good to be true." Concluding that the visitors weren't sensitive to the price of the handset, we went in the other direction by A/B testing *higher* prices. The winning page featured two higher-priced premium versions of the phone alongside the standard product. We then obtained a further win by offering optional upsells including accessories, insurance, call credit, and 24-hour customer support. So not only did A/B testing save the company from pointlessly destroying its margins, but it revealed an unexpected opportunity for growing the profits.

4. You never need to make hard decisions

Most companies run according to the following process:

Get Idea → Decide Whether to Implement It → Implement It.

A/B testing allows you to postpone the decision-making until you know the correct answer, at which point the decision is a no-brainer:

Get Idea → Implement It (as a Test) → Decide Whether to Keep It.

A/B testing thus eradicates the laborious decision-making stage, allowing companies to move faster. Endless pontification about "Should we do it?" is replaced with a simple "Let's test it and find out!"

Testing is the stopwatch; your website is the sprinter

Whichever type of testing you use, the software won't tell you *what* to test.

Unfortunately, that's the most important part. Roger Longbotham said, "What you place upon the statistical framework is what ultimately determines the attractiveness of your test results."

As with all tools, A/B testing is subject to the equation "GI → GO," which stands for "Garbage In leads to Garbage Out." In other words, if you put garbage into an A/B test, you'll get garbage out of it (albeit optimized garbage).

The A/B testing software is to CRO what a stopwatch is to a sprinter. The stopwatch doesn't make the sprinter any faster. It just measures the sprinter's performance, and tells them what is their personal best.

That's where CRO expertise comes into play. Just as GI → GO, also AI → AO (*A* being *Awesomeness*). This book will give you loads of great insights, ideas, and awesomeness to put into your tests.

Let's improve your website's personal best.

So what is CRO?

Back in 2005, when we worked in-house, we tried hard to outsource conversion. It turned out to be impossible. There were many vendors, but each pushed its own solution:

- The live chat companies claimed that live chat was the answer.
- The analytics companies claimed that analytics software was the answer.
- The usability companies claimed that usability was the answer.

- The multivariate testing vendors claimed that multivariate testing software was the answer.
- The copywriters claimed that copywriting was the answer.
- The eye-tracking companies claimed that eye-tracking was the answer.

And so on.

What we wanted was an independent advisor who was effectively a "hub" for conversion, who had used all of the services, who was completely impartial, and who knew how to get the best results.

We ended up doing it ourselves. As a result, we learned what worked. We now spend all of our time designing pages that convert—and then we put our necks on the line by insisting that we test our creations, to prove that we've measurably improved things. Over the past ten years, we have tried an enormous number of techniques, some of which were real gems. We have pulled together the best ones (along with practical, easy ways to get them done) and added many techniques that we developed ourselves. At each stage, we have shared our findings on our blog, which has rewarded us by attracting kindred spirits, people who share our passion. Hopefully, you'll be one of them.

We coined the term *conversion rate optimization* (CRO) in 2007 to describe this process of pulling together all of the available tools, techniques, and skills—with the goal of improving a website's conversion rates. CRO takes the guesswork out of creating highly profitable websites. It's a series of strategies and activities that allow you to achieve significant increases in profits from your website easily and reliably. User testing and A/B testing software allow you to carry out tests; CRO tells you *what* to test, by revealing how to create webpages that convert your visitors.

Strictly speaking, CRO is web design done right. It's making a page that is perfectly designed to sell, or get sign-ups, or get downloads, or whatever the page is there for. Even ten years later, though, the practice of CRO looks so different from how most web design is carried out that it still warrants having a separate name.

(Few people appreciate) why CRO is the most important activity for your business— and your career

Many companies start doing CRO without realizing its true potential. In this chapter, you will discover the three benefits of CRO that can drive your company into an economic "virtuous circle" of growth.

Benefit 1: The obvious one—CRO gets you more customers, free

The obvious reason to improve your conversion rate is that you want more customers without having to spend a penny more on advertising.

Your *revenue* is equal to...

- your *visitors* multiplied by...
- your *conversion rate* (the percentage of your visitors that turn into customers) multiplied by...
- the *lifetime customer spend* (the amount that each of them spends with you):

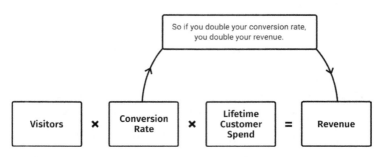

Benefit 1: Doubling your conversion rate doubles your revenue.

So if you double your conversion rate, you double your revenue. (Whenever we say "double" in this chapter, it's to make the examples easy to understand. But, as you'll see, even a small increase can result in one heck of an office party. We highly recommend you carry out the calculations for your own business. They can be eye-opening.)

But CRO has other, even better benefits...

Benefit 2: Your profit is even more sensitive to your conversion rate than your revenue is

Your profit is your revenue minus all your costs:

Profit = Revenue – Costs

When you double your conversion rate, all your costs don't double:

- Your variable costs do double (by definition). This includes all costs that scale in proportion to the number of units sold, including the cost of goods sold, the costs of direct labor, distribution, and customer support.
- But your ad costs remain the same.
- And your fixed costs stay the same (by definition).

As a result, your profit increases disproportionately. Sometimes profoundly. The following diagram shows how a doubling of conversion rate can cause the profit to multiply by four times:

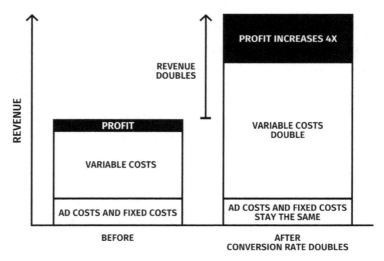

Benefit 2: An increase in conversion rate has a disproportionate effect on profit.

The effect can be even greater. For some companies, a small increase in conversion rate can mean the difference between suffering a loss and making a profit.

Benefit 3 (an even more exciting one): CRO opens up floods of traffic

Once your conversion rate has increased, you're more profitable. It pays to sacrifice some of that profit into increasing your advertising bid prices—which can dramatically increase your number of customers. You can outbid your competitors and profitably dominate all the advertising space in your market.

Many of our clients find that CRO unlocks marketing opportunities that were previously prohibitively expensive, allowing them to get loads of new customers.

For startups and small-to-medium sized businesses, CRO is often the catalyst that enables them to start advertising, profitably, in PPC, magazines, newspapers, direct mail, radio, and TV. Clients also become able to pay affiliates more—which wins the affiliates over from their competitors. The principle even applies to SEO: if a company will generate twice as much revenue from the number-one spot, it can afford to spend twice as much to capture it.

This principle is so extreme that many advertising agencies pay us to work on their clients' websites, because they understand that CRO allows their clients to profitably increase their ad spends. With the right combination of CRO and traffic buying, you can displace competitors for good.

Benefit 1 × Benefit 2 × Benefit 3 = The Power Law of CRO

Here's the best bit: Benefits 1, 2 and 3 are multiplicative. Which means your profit has a power-law relationship to your conversion rate. (That is, your profit is equal to your conversion rate to the power of something—maybe squared, cubed, or even more.)

Looking at the equations from above, you can see why:

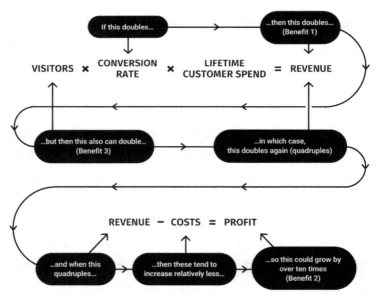

The Power Law of CRO, which explains why so many of our clients have won awards for fast growth.

Of course, the multipliers depend on the financials of the business. You can see how your own profits would be affected by an increase in conversion rate by modeling different scenarios in a spreadsheet.

Incredibly, that's not the end of it. As the number of orders grows, economies of scale kick in. These further increase the amount you can afford to spend on getting more customers.

CRO is a virtuous circle. The world's leading web companies all focus on it—on user experience, conversion flows, network effects, and customer journeys.

Without doing CRO, it's impossible to win.

Why CRO is a great career choice

In our experience, the best career strategy is to (1) **Create more value.** CRO allows you to reliably do this, and then (2) **Prove you've done so.** A/B testing allows you to do this.

As such, CRO makes for a fantastic career choice. There's a serious shortage of people who have proof that they can grow businesses. Amazingly, most people's résumés have no quantifiable evidence that they have ever created value. Thanks to CRO, many of our clients, followers, and team members have incredibly impressive success stories on their résumés.

Plus, if you're anything like us, you'll find it endlessly fascinating.

Reasons to start CRO now
The first-mover advantage

As long as you have a higher *profit-per-visitor* than your competitors do, then every day you'll have a slight unfair economic advantage over them.

The wider you make that gap, the faster you accelerate ahead. That gap becomes a moat that makes your business robust against competitors' attacks.

If your competitors aren't focusing on CRO already, they will be soon, because the market will keep getting more competitive.

Every day you're ahead, you have an unfair advantage—the wind is in your sails. Every day you are behind, you have an unfair disadvantage—you're playing catch-up.

The difference depends on how soon you start, and how fast you move.

Does your business depend on free traffic?

If your web business depends on free traffic from search engines or social media sites, you'll get the following additional benefits:

- Because CRO enables you to profitably advertise in different media, your business will become much more stable. You'll no longer be hooked on free traffic and no longer at the whim of a search engine algorithm change.
- CRO will make your website customer-centric, so your customers will like you more and stay with you for longer. It also means other websites are more likely to link to yours.

Why doubling a website's conversion rate is easier than it sounds

What's your current conversion rate? Five percent? Ten? Don't know? A 5% conversion rate means that of every twenty visitors to your site, nineteen walk away empty-handed. Do you really believe you couldn't lower that number to eighteen out of twenty?

Look at it another way: To double your conversion rate, you just need to increase the conversion rate of your

- ads by 19%;
- landing page by 19%;
- shopping cart by 19%; and
- checkout by 19%.

(The figure is 19%, not 25%, because each improvement compounds upon the previous one.) These increases may sound daunting, but to increase your landing page's conversion rate by 19%, for example, you would have to make just a 1.76% improvement to ten aspects of your landing page:

- Your company's tagline
- Your headline
- Your introductory text
- Your offer
- Your guarantee
- Your picture

- Your readability
- Your usability
- Your navigation
- Your products
- Your pricing
- Your offers
- Your premium
- Your testimonials
- Your call-to-action
- Your site layout
- Your return policy

And the list goes on...

Does a 25% increase sound more achievable now?

Also, don't be daunted by the number of techniques described in this book. If you did everything in it, you'd probably be the best marketer in the world. A single breakthrough can double your conversion rate. The most important thing is to take action.

Choose your role models wisely: Take inspiration from this awe-inspiring story of how one of our clients went from zero to half a billion dollars

We recently sorted through some old business cards from a conference we spoke at. We came across the following card, which had some interesting notes on it:

Notes from our first conversation with Mike Lee of MyFitnessPal.

Our founder Karl had spoken at the conference. After the talk, he was approached by an entrepreneur called Mike Lee. Mike didn't have a business card handy, so Karl wrote notes on one of his own cards.

Mike mentioned that he loved our articles. His company, MyFitnessPal, had created a smartphone app for counting calories. The company had just begun, but Mike was a fan of our articles and was already optimizing his business using multivariate testing.

Mike and his brother and cofounder, Albert, subsequently hired us to help MyFitnessPal grow even faster.

Mike and Albert recently sold MyFitnessPal for just under half a billion dollars.

Some people think that CRO is an activity to do "when we get round to it."

Successful companies start immediately.

In fact, successful web companies do many things

differently. Their behavior is startlingly different from the unsuccessful companies. In the following chapter, we describe three of the key differences—differences so profound that just by following them you'll gain a huge advantage.

Why the world's top websites are winning (and how yours can too)

As far as we are aware, no other company has had the privilege of designing pages for as many of the world's top 500 websites as we have. We say privilege because these companies are, by definition, already great at creating websites, and many of them wouldn't normally ask an external company to design pages for them.

When we look at how those companies improve their websites, it's striking how their practices have almost *nothing* in common with the way that most other companies do it. Their approach is perhaps best described as "Scientific Web Design." In this chapter, you will learn the three principles by which Scientific Web Design differs from most other web design, and we explain why it's much more effective.

Principle 1: The top companies design for function, not aesthetics

Take a look at the following two hammers:

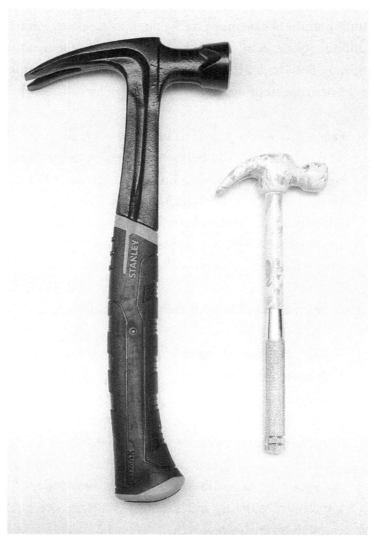

The hammer on the left is popular with professionals. The one on the right belongs to Karl's mother.

Both hammers have been meticulously designed, but for different goals. Karl's mother's hammer was designed for beauty. The Stanley hammer was designed for hammering. They represent two approaches to design:

1. Aesthetic: Karl's mother's hammer represents good design to people who believe that design means "optimize for beauty." It's not good for hammering, so Karl's mother uses her other hammer instead.
2. Functional: The Stanley hammer represents good design to people who believe that design means "optimize for the product's core function."

Similarly, there are two approaches to web design:

1. Aesthetic: Most web agencies design for beauty, paying little more than lip service toward the goals of the business and its customers.
2. Functional: In our opinion, good web design means understanding your visitors—and your business—deeply, then designing to meet both of their needs. And by *deeply*, we mean not obeying an executive who says, "I know my customers," but instead gaining deep insights through extensive research.

Which approach is most effective? Take a look at the homepages of Google, eBay, Amazon, Craigslist, LinkedIn, Facebook, Wikipedia, YouTube, and other leading websites and decide for yourself. Are they designed for beauty, or does their form follow their function?

It amazes us how few people have noticed this.

To be clear, *it's fine to optimize for beauty if your insights indicate that your visitors will buy more as a result.* At that point, functional design and aesthetic design become the same thing, and you should test making your website more beautiful. The mistake happens when companies think that pure aesthetics are a substitute for research and testing.

Scientific Web Design is functional.

Why not design for function *and* aesthetics?

Some people ask why they shouldn't optimize for function *and* aesthetics. Even if their visitors are perfectly happy with the current appearance of the website, what's the harm in being beautiful regardless?

It's like asking **"What's the harm in giving an Olympic sprinter an egg and spoon to carry while he runs?"** They don't realize that beauty, like an egg and spoon, tends to slow progress to a crawl.

One of our first clients had one of the most beautiful, polished sites we had ever seen. We first noticed a problem when we asked the head developer to italicize a particular word. "That's not just a fifteen-minute job," he replied, "It will have to wait till next week." We were amazed. We had just come from working in-house, where we had tripled our employer's sales in twelve months. We were used to making changes quickly. Putting a word into italics would have taken us sixty seconds. We had taken that agility for granted.

Imagine if your site were as easy to edit as Wikipedia, Google Docs, or Justin Jackson's article "This Is a Web Page" (which we urge you to read). How much more work would you get done? How quickly could you iterate? Typical web marketers could edit a Wikipedia page in one minute, but would take at least a day to make a similar change to their own site. That's over a thousand times longer. Much of that time difference is because their own site is more complicated for aesthetic reasons: Fonts are substituted, decorative images are included, layouts are complicated, and ornamental graphics are added. The technical burden soon becomes immense: changes must be checked on multiple devices running multiple browsers on multiple operating systems; plug-ins conflict; fonts don't render...

...and before long, you're no longer outraged that it takes seven days—seven days!—to turn a word into italics.

Meanwhile, Facebook has pushed live several *thousand* more changes.

If your website is already more beautiful than Amazon's, and your customers are happy with its appearance, are you sure that the best way to grow your business is to make it more beautiful—or have you just run out of ideas? Beauty can lead to sluggishness, and sluggishness can lead to economic death.

If you do make your website more beautiful, ensure your designs are minimalist—visually and technically. Keep them elegantly simple and easy to update. And don't forget that—like the Stanley hammer—good functional design has a beauty of its own.

Principle 2: The top companies carry out experiments on their websites

When top companies change their websites, they measure the effects of the changes, using A/B testing software or some other type of experimental technique. We have already described the benefits of A/B testing. The following quotes may be useful if you're trying to persuade your company to adopt a culture of testing:

"Being able to figure out quickly what works and what doesn't can mean the difference between survival and extinction." —Hal Varian, Google Chief Economist

"If you double the number of experiments you do per year you're going to double your inventiveness." —Jeff Bezos, CEO of Amazon

Here's another great quote by Jeff Bezos:

"...successful invention, if you want to do a lot of that, you basically have to increase your rate of experimentation and that you can think of as a process—how do you go about organizing your systems, your people, all of your assets, your own daily life and how you spend time, how do you increase those things to increase your rate of experimentation?"

Principle 3: For reasons that are subtle, the top companies make frequent, incremental changes, and rarely (if ever) have huge site redesigns

"Every work day Facebook is safely updated with hundreds of changes including bug fixes, new features, and product improvements. Given hundreds of engineers, thousands of changes every week and hundreds of millions of users we have worldwide, this task seems like it should be impossible."
—Chuck Rossi, Facebook's Release Engineering Manager

The top companies update their sites frequently—often weekly and sometimes daily. The changes are usually improvements to parts of pages rather than complete page redesigns or website redesigns. If you update your site in incremental iterations like this, you get three benefits:

1. **You get to see what's working** (and what's not working) on a granular level.
2. **Your site-improvement process stays nimble** because it's always in use and is not mothballed until the next mega-redesign.
3. **You decrease the amount of work-in-progress** (work that has been carried out, but is not yet at a stage where it can bear fruit).

Work-in-progress is the toadstool of business; it looks harmless but is poisonous. For example,

- Any **work-in-progress is wasted money** until it sees the light of day.
- **Managing work-in-progress is work in itself**, particularly with large projects. Large projects constipate companies.
- **Problems aren't seen until the eleventh hour.** Some companies hire us after having had a sitewide redesign that actually decreased their conversion rate. In fact, at the time of writing, we are rescuing a website for which one of our clients had paid tens of millions of dollars. You might expect that a website that cost that much would perform extremely well. However, we are redesigning it page by page, and our pages are considerably outperforming the existing ones.
- **The longer a project takes, the greater the expectation for a massive win** once the redesign goes live. This results in the additional inertia of deliberation, double- and triple-checking, and design-by-committee, all of which erode speed (a dangerous practice in highly competitive markets). It's no surprise then, that:
- **Many projects are never completed.**

That's why Scientific Web Design entails carrying out frequent, iterative changes.

Why do some people willfully ignore these principles?

Some people choose *not* to follow the three principles of Scientific Web Design, for several reasons:

- Some people avoid accountability.
- People who work for agencies may not want their performance to be measured soon and frequently. There's good money in quoting for huge **white-elephant projects**, delaying that moment of truth until all the money is in the bank.
- To uninitiated buyers, **aesthetic design is easier to sell**. Whether it's hammers or websites, some people buy beauty.

How to follow all three principles—and why it makes life hard in the short term but easier in the long term

The three principles of Scientific Web Design are embedded into our methodology as follows:

- First, analyze your website and visitors. Through intensive research, identify the biggest opportunities for improvement.
- Next, implement the changes in frequent, small, targeted iterations.
- Put your neck on the line (like we do) by insisting that

the changes be A/B tested to prove (or disprove) that they have grown the business.

This makes life challenging, because of course not every experiment results in a win; but there's a strength in it too: you get immediate feedback, so you discover what works (and what doesn't) for your specific marketplace.

That's rare in business.

By taking this approach, your internal processes over time get reengineered for speed and profits—a hallmark of the top online businesses.

How can you benefit from Scientific Web Design?

By the fact that you are reading this, you are probably already persuaded of the principles of Scientific Web Design. If so, here's what you can do:

- **If you are a marketer or designer**, ensure that you follow the three success principles: Design pages that fulfill their primary purpose, measure and test everything you create, and minimize your work-in-progress. Learn how to make websites ultra-effective.
- **If you are a manager, director, or company owner** and you are struggling to persuade your team to show any interest in CRO, first set the "ground rules": Insist that they always follow the three principles. (1) Design pages that fulfill their primary purpose. (2) Measure and test everything you create. (3) Minimize your work-in-

progress. Pushing conversion knowledge upon someone is futile unless they are hungry for it. By setting the "rules of the game" (insisting that your team follows the three principles), you align their goals with those of your business, and your team will devour any information that will be useful to them. Then, when they measurably grow your business, your challenge becomes to pay them enough to keep them. Conversion skills are in short supply.

· **Whoever you are**, spread the word. We estimate that, worldwide, fewer than 1% of marketing decisions follow the principles of Scientific Web Design. Much of the web-design industry actively avoids them. So when you see people violating the principles described in this chapter, speak out. Write your own articles about this subject. Be the child who dares to tell the emperor that he's wearing no clothes (and is carrying an egg and spoon). You don't need to have a scientific background— you just need to have the diligence and discipline to follow the principles. And when you encounter people who dare to follow the principles of Scientific Web Design, encourage and support them. They haven't chosen the easy path.

Why you should **avoid meek tweaking** (and not just because it sounds creepy)

Just because your changes are going to be incremental and

frequent doesn't mean they should be minor or trivial. In fact, the biggest mistake people make when optimizing their websites is what we call "meek tweaking." They set up A/B testing software, then they make daft changes. They change button colors and shuffle items around the page, just because they read that it worked for someone else. They do the Garbage In → Garbage Out thing.

The following graph explains why that approach is more harmful than it sounds.

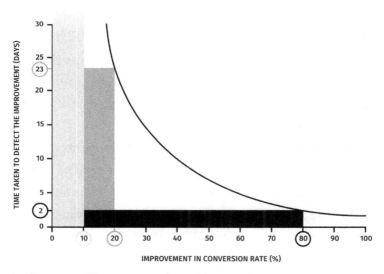

In A/B tests, small improvements take much longer to detect.

The horizontal axis shows the improvement you are looking to detect. The vertical axis shows the time it will take to detect that improvement.

The curved line shows how long it will take for an A/B

test to reach completion. It's for a page that gets 300 views/day (that's about 9,000 views/month). The shape of the curve would be similar (just higher or lower) for other traffic volumes.

Imagine that you have just designed a new version of such a page, and your new version has an **80% higher** conversion rate than the existing version. As you can see in the graph, the time taken to detect that improvement would be just **two days.**

Whereas if your new version was only **20% better** than the existing page, the A/B test would take **twenty-three days** to reach completion.

In other words, **to detect an improvement that's a quarter as large** (20% compared with 80%), **then your A/B test would take over *ten times* as long** (twenty-three days compared with two days).

If you were looking to detect a **10% improvement,** then the A/B test would take **several *months*** to conclude.

The moral of the story is that **small improvements take ages to detect,** disproportionately and counterintuitively so.

So you should **aim for bold, targeted changes,** because

1. **Each change gets you more profit** (an 80% improvement gives four times the benefit of a 20% improvement, obviously).
2. **It's more fun and interesting.**
3. **It's *much* quicker.**

Whereas if you're doing what we call *meek tweaking*—making small, arbitrary changes, then

1. You tend to get no wins. **Your A/B tests never reach conclusion.**
2. This becomes **disheartening**, and you lose motivation.
3. You **lose the buy-in** from all the other people in your company whom you persuaded that A/B testing was going to be a good idea.

DiPS (Diagnose → Problem → Solution) thrashes meek tweaking

Most marketers do things to their websites that they'd never do to their bodies.

The most common causes of death in people are heart disease, cancer, stroke, respiratory infection, diabetes, and dementia. However, on seeing that list, only a fool would rush to a pharmacy and start taking medication against all of those ailments, wolfing down pills for diseases they don't have. Such behavior would cause more harm than good. Instead, sensibly, when someone is ill, they go to a physician who first diagnoses what's wrong and only then prescribes the most relevant remedy.

That may sound obvious for health, but it's not what people do with their websites. Most web marketers run straight to the "marketing pharmacy" and cram their webpages with every possible remedy. Then they wonder why they have a website that's cluttered and converts no better—or even worse—than the previous version. It's marketing malpractice. Their visitors had specific objections, but instead of overcoming those objections, the marketers filled their pages with irrelevant distractions. They should be struck off.

Your visitors' attention is limited. You must treat it preciously.

DiPS: A formula for success

The following approach to conversion is *much* more effective than the one described above. We call it Diagnose–Problem–Solution (DiPS for short). DiPS is the web-marketing equivalent of the physician doing tests to diagnose what is wrong, then analyzing the test data to identify the problem, and then coming up with an appropriate solution.

To implement DiPS, you first need to carry out research to diagnose your website's problems. You'll need to understand a lot about your visitors and how they interact with your website.

Conversion solutions are highly targeted; the problems are like locks—the solutions like keys

Here's an example to illustrate why DiPS is so effective. And why the alternative—blindly applying best practices—is so ineffective.

Imagine that a company, ABC Corps, had just launched a new product, the ABCmatic.

Would you buy one? Probably not, for one of the following reasons:

1. You don't know **what it does.**
2. You know what it does, but you don't know **why you'd need one.**
3. You aren't convinced that **it will do what it claims to do.**
4. You don't know whether it's **compatible with your existing technology.**
5. You think it's **too expensive.**
6. You **don't trust the company.** You've never heard of them before.
7. You are **going to think about it.**

If you don't know what the ABCmatic does, ABC Corps would have to explain what it does. Would a guarantee help instead? No. Would a lower price help instead? Not at all. Would testimonials help? No. None of those things would help one iota. The *only* thing that could advance your decision is an explanation of what the ABCmatic does—such as "ABCmatic allows you to manage your computer's memory." In fact, all those other solutions would merely reduce the chance that you'd ever find the paragraph that explains what the product does. The problem is like a lock, and the solution is like a key.

Now, imagine that you understand what the ABCmatic does, but can't understand why that would benefit you. Would a guarantee help? No! Would a lower price help?

No! Would a price discount help? No! The only thing that would advance your decision is an explanation of how the features relate to benefits that you care about—such as an explanation that "The ABCmatic helps to clear your computer's memory cache, so your computer runs up to twice as fast." That would do the job. Nothing else would.

And so, for each objection, you need to display a clear counterobjection.

- If visitors don't know **what it does**, then **explain what it does**.
- If visitors know what it does, but they don't know **why they'd need one**, then **explain the benefits**.
- If visitors aren't convinced that **it will do what it claims to do**, then **add proof**.
- If visitors don't know whether it's **compatible with your existing technology**, then **explain the compatibility details**.
- If visitors think it's **too expensive**, then **justify the price**.
- If visitors **don't trust the company**, then **show evidence that the company is trustworthy**.
- If visitors are **going to think about it**, then **provide reasons to act promptly**.

It's the same with every single page element on a website. Every image, every word has a very specific purpose—usually to create a thought in the visitors' minds that will move them closer to taking action. Guarantees, for example, are mechanisms that have two very specific functions: to reduce risk and to demonstrate that the company is confident in its claims. So guarantees work only when risk and proof are issues. In other situations, they make no difference. *Negative headlines* are another example of a mechanism. Negative headlines (such as "7 Mistakes to Avoid When Choosing a CRM") work when the visitors have decided that they'll do something (in this case, choose a CRM) and their main thought is "How can I avoid making the wrong decision?" In such cases, negative headlines work great; otherwise, they don't.

Most marketers know some conversion mechanisms, but few understand each mechanism's function. So they litter pages with "best practices"—a practice that's far from best.

The best marketers create funnels that counter each objection at the exact moment that the visitors are thinking it. And the only way to do that is to understand the visitors well.

The best marketers find out—not guess—exactly why their visitors aren't currently converting.

If only there were some great techniques for finding out...

Diagnosis

The ultimate guide to tools and techniques to understand how your website can be improved

A **goldmine** of techniques

In 2008, we published the most comprehensive article about how to understand your website's visitors. Back then, there were hardly any tools for doing it: our list contained just fourteen. As evidence of how much the web has changed since then, this section contains 200 resources—software, techniques and UX tools for finding out exactly why your potential customers aren't converting.

It's pure gold.

Why it pays to **understand your visitors**

It's hard to delight people if you don't know them.

Winning web businesses understand their customers better than their competitors do.

Fortune magazine described our approach as "a combination of multivariate statistical analysis and good old-fashioned detective work." This section is about the detective work.

So what do you need to know about your visitors? You need to know

- what makes them tick;
- what stops them from ticking more often;
- how you can increase their dollars-per-tick (we might be straining the "tick" analogy here).

At the very least, you need to understand why most of them leave without buying.

Unfortunately, those nonconverting visitors come and go without a trace. How can you find out what they wanted? How do you know what would have persuaded them to take action?

If you owned a real-life bricks-and-mortar store, this would be easy: You'd hear their objections. You'd be able to ask questions. You'd hear what they muttered as they headed for the door.

Capturing the voice of the customer is more difficult on the web, but it can be done. It's what our Research Department does every day. Over the past ten years, we have carried out research for hundreds of companies. We have used every type of tool. (We often use whichever tools our clients are already using, so we are forced to know them all.)

We are also constantly testing out new ways of using the tools. What's the best question to ask visitors when they exit a page? And how do you word that question to get the highest response rate?

We know it, we've tested it, and in this section we share all the details. We will describe the tools and techniques that we have found to be the most useful—those that generate the most "insights per minute." Each technique provides insight into a different aspect of your visitors' behavior— including what the visitors want, what they like, how they make decisions, and what they don't like. Together, they create a clear picture of how you can improve your website's performance and profits.

How we've categorized the following techniques

It used to be that each software solution carried out a specific function. Now, they all tend to be turning into all-purpose suites, making them hard to categorize. We have grouped each software solution into **the functionality for which we most often use it.**

Mobile web usage has skyrocketed, but the tools for understanding visitors have been slow to catch up. It's finally happening, though. Throughout this series, we will label some of the tools as being **"mobile-friendly."** That doesn't mean that the others aren't; it just means that either the tool has been specifically built for mobile, or that we have experience using the tool on mobile devices, and it works well.

Some of the techniques require a lot of visitors. So before we dive in, let's take a quick tour of which of them you should focus on if you have a low-traffic website.

Techniques for **low-traffic websites**
Why conversion is hard for low-traffic websites

If you are a startup or a small company, you are in a chicken-and-egg situation:

- To afford **visitors**, you need a good **conversion rate.**
- But it's hard to improve your **conversion rate** if you have no **visitors.**

Low-traffic websites have two problems:

Problem 1: How can you understand your visitors?

For example, how can find out what's stopping them from taking action? It's not easy when there aren't many of them to ask. Tumbleweed can't tell you how it feels.

Problem 2: How can you measure what works? High-traffic websites rely on A/B tests to measure whether their changes make a statistically significant difference. But A/B tests often don't reach significance when there isn't enough traffic.

If you're feeling overwhelmed, take heart in the knowledge that every successful company has had to pass through this stage at one point.

We'll tackle the first of those problems now. We'll address Problem 2 later, in the chapter on A/B testing.

The solution to Problem 1: The techniques you should use to understand your visitors if your website doesn't get much traffic

Some of the techniques we mention in this section rely upon a website getting lots of traffic. Some surveys, for example, typically get a completion rate of 3%. If your business is small, we recommend that you **make the most of the following techniques, which can be carried out even if your website gets just a few visitors per day.** Each of them is described in detail in the following chapters:

- **User tests** tend to be the most fruitful technique. Ask a friend—or anyone you can get your hands on—to participate. Once your website is refined enough, aim to user test it on people who are from your target demographic and psychographic.

- **Watch session recordings** of the visitors you have. Doing so will give you insight into how web visitors see your website. Plus, you'll see your creation through fresh eyes.
- **Speak to salespeople** (what we call "VOC Aggregators")—people who have sold face-to-face the same type of product—or similar products.
- **Analyze competitors' websites.** Or, if you don't have any obvious competitors, look at companies that are successful within adjacent fields. For example, if you sell B2B software, look at other B2B software vendors.
- **Add your phone number** prominently to the top of every page. Even if you have no plans to encourage phone calls on an ongoing basis, it can help to get at least a few of them. In fact, you may be able to charm your early callers into becoming long-term user testers.
- **Increase the incentives** for visitors to complete surveys. The more you offer as an incentive, the higher percentage of responses you are likely to get.

It's easier to learn CRO by working on high-traffic websites

Low-traffic websites aren't the best places to learn the craft of CRO; it's easier to learn by working on websites that get lots of traffic.

So, if you want to become world-class at CRO, you would benefit from finding an opportunity to work on a high-traffic website. If the low-traffic website in question is yours, and you can't afford to take a sabbatical working on a high-traffic website, then you may want to hire someone who has.

With high-traffic websites, you get exposed to fire hoses of feedback. Feedback fire hoses are valuable for two reasons. In the short term, they allow you to iterate and improve what you're working on. But they also hone your craft. The top performers in many fields of endeavor are those who have, at some point in their careers, been exposed to fire hoses of feedback. Most successful movie comedians, for example, developed their comedy intuition by performing night after night in front of live audiences, getting instant feedback on every word, movement, and gesture they made. Most successful bands began their careers playing in front of live audiences, learning—on a second-by-second basis—what audiences liked and disliked. So if you want to become great at conversion, seek opportunities to work on high-traffic websites. Ideally, you want to work in a company that's big enough to have loads of traffic and agile enough to allow you to move fast. In doing so, you'll quickly develop a knack of knowing what will convert—and what won't.

Then, when you've learned the craft, you'll find it much easier to grow a low-traffic website.

Right, on to the techniques...

Installing a tag manager (to help you activate and deactivate tags without having to speak with your IT department each time)

This section will no doubt persuade you to install multiple tools on your website. You may get tired of asking your developers to activate, manage, and deactivate tags. So before we continue, you may benefit from installing a tag-management solution. Tag-management solutions provide marketers with an easy-to-use interface that doesn't require the user to have IT skills or IT permissions.

Tools for tag management

Google Tag Manager is very popular. Alternatives include Adobe Activation Core Service, Conversant Tag Manager, Ensighten, IBM Digital Data Exchange, Qubit Opentag, Rakuten Storm Tag Manager, SuperTag by Datalicious, Tag Manager by Impact Radius, TagCommander, Tealium iQ, and UberTags.

Diagnose by…using web analytics (to track where your visitors came from, and which links they clicked on)

Web analytics software gives you details about the visitors to your website—where they came from, and which links they clicked on once they arrived. It's essential for CRO, but it tells only a small part of the story. It's like the closed-circuit TV cameras in a supermarket. They give an aerial view of where visitors entered the store, but they don't reveal *why* the visitors came. They show the path that visitors took through the store, but they don't reveal what the visitors were thinking. They show you exactly where and when the visitors left the store, but not why. Or what to do about it. For that, you'll need qualitative tools, which are described later.

You'll find web analytics most useful in the early stages of a project, when you are seeking to identify on which pages to start work. It will also inform the pages on which you should implement the tools described in the rest of the chapters in this section. If a page gets no visitors, then changing it will have no effect. Nor will changing a page that already has 100% conversion rate. Web analytics software will help you to identify the arteries of the website—the high-traffic flows that lead to successful conversions. Along with other tools, it can also help you to spot the aspects of those flows that are currently underperforming.

Tools for web analytics

Despite being free, Google Analytics is a sophisticated and powerful web analytics suite. It is sufficient for most websites, and most of our clients use it or its enterprise equivalent, Google Analytics 360.

Google Analytics alternatives include Adobe Analytics, Webtrends, Quantcast Measure, Woopra, Piwik, and Flurry Analytics specializes in mobile apps.

Kissmetrics and Mixpanel provide additional functionality that can be useful to conversion marketers. Cohort reports, for example, show how groups of visitors behave over a long period. Amplitude helps marketers to understand how users behave within a website or app.

Diagnose by...capturing easy-to-interpret click maps (to see exactly where visitors clicked—even if it wasn't on a link)

Whereas web analytics software tells you what links your visitors click on, click-mapping software shows you which parts of your pages your visitors click on. There's a subtle difference: click-mapping software shows you clicks even if they weren't on a link. This information is displayed as a "heat map," like this:

Crazy Egg's confetti map shows exactly where visitors clicked—even if it wasn't on a link.

Click-mapping offers several advantages:

1. It will reveal **things that are getting clicked but are not clickable.** You'll discover that visitors are clicking on parts of the page that aren't links but perhaps should be. For example, if you discover visitors are clicking on a product photo, you may choose to allow the picture to be magnified, or you may decide readers want to read more information about it. Similarly, they may wrongly believe that a particular graphic is navigation.

2. It will also reveal, at a glance, **which parts of the page are getting the most attention.** This can be particularly useful when you're showing the data to people who aren't experienced in web analytics.

3. If several of the links on your page lead to the same URL—for example, if there are three links to a particular product page—click-mapping will show you **which of the links your visitors clicked on.** This is technically possible with analytics, but requires some set-up.

4. Have you ever wondered **how far visitors scroll down your pages**? Many click-mapping tools can give you the answer, in the form of easy-to-interpret scroll maps. If some of your pages are long, scroll maps can reveal which parts of the page get the most attention (based on the average viewing time). This can be great for identifying which parts of your page are most important to your visitors. If one of your pages has a "false bottom"—a gap in the design that appears to visitors to be the bottom

of the page—then a scroll map will reveal that visitors aren't scrolling. (You then need to work out whether that's because they didn't realize that the page could be scrolled, or because they weren't interested enough to scroll.)

We recommend you study click-mapping reports of your most important pages (in terms of revenue and traffic) and of any pages you feel may have usability issues.

Of course, most heat maps show many things that are predictable, but that's not why you should use heat maps. Ignore the predictable heat and look for the anomalies.

Tools for click-mapping

We often use Crazy Egg (mobile-friendly), Hotjar (mobile-friendly), Clicktale (mobile-friendly) and several A/B testing tools that include similar functionality. Other alternatives include Fullstory, Inspectlet, Decibel Insight (mobile-friendly), Jaco, Lucky Orange, MouseStats, Ptengine, UsabilityTools, userTrack, and Zeerat.

Diagnose by...using session-recording tools
(to see videos of visitors' screens and more)

Hotjar's session recordings allow you to see how your visitors struggled their way through your website.

Web analytics software is concerned mostly with the movement of visitors between pages. Session-recording tools can be a great complement, revealing what visitors did on each page, by capturing each visitor's keystrokes and mouse movement.

Session-recording tools can be useful in the following ways:

1. **Replay sessions:** Watch movies of your visitors' screens as they use your website. You can view visitors' browsing sessions as videos, as if you were looking over their shoulders. You can choose which video to watch based

on attributes such as the visitor's country of origin, how much time they spend on the site, or the number of pages they visited. You may choose to watch videos of visitors who appear to be struggling—for example, those who visit the same page several times.

2. **Get a feel for how people use websites:** Session-recording tools are not a substitute for carrying out user tests, which are described later. However, watching a few videos will give you a better idea of how people interact with websites.

3. **See errors:** The software can display a report of errors that users have encountered.

4. **Analyze funnels:** Get to see where your visitors are dropping off. Clicktale, in particular, makes it easy to study funnels for opportunities.

5. **See scroll maps:** Scroll maps reveal how far down your page visitors scrolled.

Tools for recording sessions

Clicktale (mobile-friendly) pioneered session-recording software. Alternatives include Hotjar (mobile-friendly), Inspectlet, UsabilityTools, UserReplay, SessionCam, FullStory, Decibel Insight (mobile-friendly), and Mouseflow. (Each tool tends to have multiple functions, so our choice of tool often depends on the combination of features and functions that a particular client requires. Also, some of our clients already have a tool installed when we begin the project.)

Some companies—such as those in financial services—are regulated as to how their data must be stored. Clicktale offers an enterprise version for such cases. IBM Tealeaf is another popular alternative for enterprises. Decibel Insight offers on-premises deployment, so you can store data in your own environment and have complete control.

Diagnose by...using form-analytics software (to identify which of your form fields are causing trouble)

Form-analytics software allows you to study how people are interacting with your forms. The software is extremely important, because visitors who interact with forms are very likely to convert. By finding out why they bail, you can unlock great profits.

The software can report on many issues, including the following:

- The **overall success** of the form: how many visitors landed on it, and what percentage of them interacted with it, tried to submit it, and successfully submitted it.
- The percentage of visitors who **dropped out** at each form field. Knowing this information allows you to fix—or remove—the form fields that are causing visitors to lose their patience and abandon your website.
- The **amount of time** that visitors spend on each field. Even if the visitors don't abandon at a particular field—maybe it's early in the form and they are still

motivated—it may fatigue them, causing them to abandon later.

- Which fields tend to get **left blank**. A blank response often indicates that a field is confusing or intimidating. Such fields reduce a visitor's resolve to complete the form.
- Which fields result in **error messages**, which the visitors then need to edit before they can resubmit the form.
- **Which browsers and devices are performing poorly.** Maybe your form is hard to use on small mobile devices.

Tools for form analytics

Options include Clicktale (mobile-friendly), Hotjar (mobile-friendly), Formisimo, Decibel Insight (mobile-friendly), SessionCam, and Inspectlet.

Diagnose by...**using live chat** (to let your visitors tell you what's wrong with your pages)

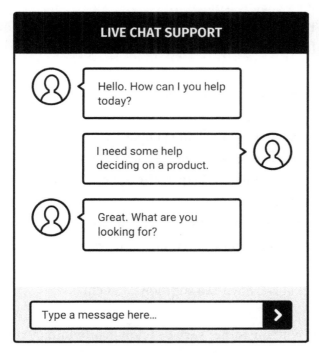

Live chat software helps in several ways: you can convert visitors via the chat conversations, you can discover their objections, and you can test your counter-objections.

Live chat can allow you to hear from visitors who wouldn't phone you. Such visitors might prefer live chat for some of the following reasons:

- They are in a public place (or at work) and don't want to be heard.

- They appreciate that, unlike phone calls, live chat doesn't cost money.
- They don't want to be stuck at the end of a phone waiting for someone to answer.
- They feel that a live chat session is less of a commitment than a phone call.

Live chat can reveal the following:

1. which **pages** are giving people problems;
2. which **products** people are asking questions about;
3. what visitors' main **questions, concerns, and objections are;**
4. which of your **answers, reassurances, and counter-objections** persuade visitors to take further action.

Live chat can have two additional benefits:

- If your customer service team is providing your live chat, you may choose to read through the transcripts of the chats regularly to find insights you can apply to your website.
- If the customer service team uses canned responses, then study them. They can be pure, field-tested copywriting gold—provided they have been refined over time to be the best responses.
- Using live chat may increase your conversion rate, by personally helping the visitors to take action.

Tools for live chat

Popular tools for live chat include Zendesk Chat, LiveChat, Drift, Freshdesk, Olark, LivePerson, HappyFox, SnapEngage, LiveAgent, Intercom (for web apps), and Comm100. Some of them, like Intercom, allow you to track, help, and convert visitors across multiple browsing sessions.

Diagnose by...**using cobrowsing** (so your visitors can share their screens with you)

Cobrowsing software allows your visitors to share their screens with a customer-support person. Cobrowsing tends to be particularly useful when you struggle to work out what your visitors are seeing—for example, if the visitor is looking at a dynamically generated page, like a page of search results or an interface in a web app.

Tools for cobrowsing

Tools for cobrowsing include Pega, Oracle Service Cloud, and Surfly.

Diagnose by...**using survey tools** (to ask your visitors and customers whatever you want to know)

To help us grow our clients' businesses, we carry out extensive research. Over ten million people have seen our surveys.

Surveys are powerful, because your customers know the answers to a surprising number of your marketing questions.

So why not ask them?

Awesome, tested questions to ask your customers

The following questions can provide invaluable insights. We recommend you identify the ones that will populate the gaps in your existing knowledge.

- **"How likely are you to recommend us to a friend or colleague?"** Answers should be on a scale of 0 (not 1) to 10. This is known as the "Net Promoter Question." It can be deceptively useful. In the chapter on lifetime customer value (LCV), you'll see the theory behind it, and details of how to analyze the data from it.
- **"In the past six months, have you criticized or spoken highly of [YourCompanyName] to a friend, colleague, or family member? If so, please give details."** This is a great way to jog the customer's memory and elicit specific criticism or specific praise. In the latter case, you might get a response that could be used as a testimonial. (If you want to use it that way, be sure to get permission first.)
- **"If you could have us create something just for you, what would it be?"** Your customers can be a good source of ideas for new products, and this question is a great way of collecting those ideas. More straightforward—but less thought-provoking—wording would be **"What other products or services should we offer?"**
- If you don't know how you differ from your competitors, there's a good chance your customers can tell you. **"How**

would you describe us to a friend?" reveals why your customers like you. Similarly, you could ask a question along the lines of the following: **"Which other options did you consider before choosing our product or service?"** or **"Why did you decide to use us?"** It's particularly important to ask questions from this group before you undertake any re-branding exercise, so you understand what your existing positioning is.

- **"Do you use us for all your [ProductType] or do you also use alternative companies? If so, why?"**
- **"Why do you use [YourCompanyName or YourProductName] rather than the alternatives?"**
- If you want your customers to use you more often, you could do worse than to ask them **"What would persuade you to use us more often?"** Can you see how survey questions can save you a lot of trial and error?
- **"How could we persuade your friends or colleagues to use us?" "If you were in charge of our company, how would you persuade people like yourself to use us?"** and **"If you were in charge of our company, how would you spread the word about us?"**

Not every answer will be valuable, but even a single gem can lead to a boost in profits.

The answer to this one question could skyrocket your sales

We have devised one question that's incredibly useful. In

fact, it almost always reveals an easy way to increase a company's sales. It works like magic on any business—online or offline.

We arrived at it after seeing a TV program about a military assault course—a series of rope swings, climbing nets, and muddy pools. The TV presenter was interviewing people who had just finished the course, asking them what had been the worst obstacle. Several of the finishers mentioned a tall wall that had been tough to climb. The scene then cut to a view of that wall, revealing that, sure enough, many people were still stuck behind the wall. After several attempts at climbing it, they were giving up and dropping out.

We wondered how we could adapt that question to sales processes, to identify the conceptual "walls" that prevent prospects from buying.

We devised the question, asked it of our clients' customers, and discovered that it has an incredible ability to identify obstacles—and hence opportunities for growth. The question is so valuable, it deserves its own page (but it's not going to get one). The question is...rabba dabba dabba (this is supposed to be a drum roll) dabba dabba dabba...TISH!

"What nearly stopped you buying from us?"

The wording can be modified depending on what your company does. It could also end with "from using us" or "from signing up."

You can also ask the question in many ways. For example, you can use a survey on your website's thank-you page or even email the customer a link to the survey. In other cases, it's worth asking the question when speaking to customers—either face-to-face or on the phone.

There are some important subtleties and realizations as to why the question works so well.

Reason 1: You put it to your customers, not to those who didn't buy from you

This might sound counterintuitive. Surely, you might think, if Alice buys one of your sports cars and Bob doesn't, it's Bob's opinions that you need to hear. But the problem with nonbuyers like Bob is that they are a mixed bunch. Some of them will be qualified to buy from you and many of them won't. For example, some Bobs just want to test drive a sports car and have no intention of buying. If you ask Bobs why they didn't buy, their responses can be red herrings; often they complain about price. The Alices, on the other hand, are (by definition) qualified prospects. And you'd like more of them.

Reason 2: Your customers have been through the entire sales funnel and your noncustomers haven't

Your customers know what they are talking about. They've paid enough attention to make a decision, so they know enough to be able to make good suggestions. A noncustomer, on the other hand, may have bailed after only a few seconds. His or her opinion—however strong—is much less likely to be accurate. When your buyers criticize you, they are likely to be right.

Reason 3: Even though your customers overcame every barrier to buying from you, they weren't oblivious to the barriers

When you ask Alice, "What nearly stopped you buying from us?" she will still remember the biggest barriers. And for every Alice who successfully overcame the barriers, you'll almost certainly find there were several people who gave up. When you remove the barrier, sales increase.

There are clear benefits to asking this question. And it works on *any* process that you'd like more people to complete.

So...what's nearly stopping you from asking it?

Other things you need to know about your customers

You need to know which of your products your customers like most, and why.

The products that are most liked aren't necessarily the ones that you sell most of. Just because a restaurant might sell a lot of lasagna doesn't mean their lasagna is well liked. In fact, it might be deterring customers from ever coming back.

By knowing which of your products is most liked, you can

- design the most effective sales funnel, so your most-liked products aren't hidden away; and
- improve your existing products, to make purchasers more likely to buy from you again.

Your survey can constantly be changing, which will allow you to keep getting deeper insights into your visitors and customers. A survey may reveal insights that you decide to explore further in subsequent surveys.

Asking questions to your noncustomers

So far, we have only discussed customers but your non-customers are a valuable source of information, too. After all, they are the ones you are trying to convert. You can ask noncustomers many of the questions above, via exit surveys, survey panels, and many other techniques, all of which we'll describe in the following chapters.

What to do if you have no one to survey

If you have no one to survey—perhaps because you're working on a startup or a product for a new market—then Google Consumer Surveys can be useful. You choose your target audience from Google's panel of users, type your questions, and then receive responses within hours. It works best for products and services that have broad appeal. Similar, but more flexible, is Pollfish.

Learn more about questions

For more about the subject of asking questions, visit our website and watch the talk "Golden questions" that reveal exactly why your visitors aren't converting (slides and video)."

Tools for surveying

We often use the following survey tools: SurveyMonkey, Google Forms (which has few features, but is agile) and Survey Gizmo. Other popular solutions include Medallia Digital (mobile-friendly), Survey Anyplace (specifically for mobile), Wufoo, Clicktools, Polldaddy, Typeform, and Uservoice. If yours is a professional services company, then CLIENTPulse is purpose-made to find out all the things you need to know.

Diagnose by...**using exit survey tools** (to ask your visitors why they didn't take action)

Visitors don't know why they abandoned until after they abandoned. Exit surveys allow you to gather insights that couldn't have been gathered any sooner.

One of the best times to capture your visitors' objections is as soon as they have them: at the moment that they leave your website. The following questions can come in useful in exit surveys:

- **Question 1:** What was the purpose of your visit?
- **Question 2:** Were you able to complete the purpose of your visit today?
- **If they answer no to Question 2, ask Question 3:** What stopped you completing the purpose of your visit today?

If your website has multiple distinct segments of visitors, you may choose to add a question that reveals the visitor's segment too.

Tools for exit surveys

iPerceptions provides a ready-made way of implementing exit surveys. You can also create them using Usabilla, Informizely, Qualaroo (mobile-friendly), Hotjar (mobile-friendly), Medallia Digital (mobile-friendly), and ForeSee.

Diagnose by...**using on-page survey tools** (to ask questions at exactly the right moment)

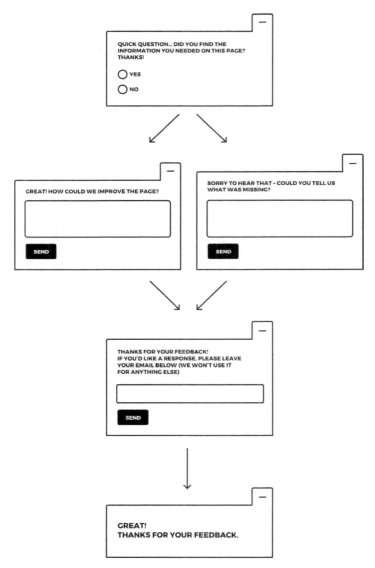

Exit surveys allow your visitors to tell you why they abandoned your website.

Some information can best be obtained by surveying your visitors while they are on a specific page. In doing so, you can ask questions at the exact moment that the visitors are thinking the thoughts you want to hear. On-page survey tools let you add surveys to the corner of a page or, more prominently, to its middle, obscuring the other content.

Several options are available:

- You can decide **what type of response** you want. You can have radio buttons, multiple-answer checkboxes, or open text fields.
- You can decide **who will participate** in the survey. For example, you could arrange to show the survey only to returning visitors who have been viewing the page for fifty seconds.
- You can ask **several questions** in one survey.
- You can **receive email notifications of responses**. Sometimes respondents ask questions to which they expect answers.

Tools for on-page surveys

We often use Qualaroo (mobile-friendly), Informizely, and Hotjar. Alternatives include Medallia Digital (mobile-friendly), Webreep, Feedback Lite, PopSurvey and WebEngage.

Diagnose by...**using a persistent "Give Feedback" button** (to allow your visitors to report issues to you)

"Give Feedback" buttons allow your visitors to leave feedback at a time of their choosing.

Have you ever been frustrated by a website, but couldn't find any way to communicate your frustrations to its creators?

Your own visitors never need to feel that way. Simply add a "Give Feedback" button to every page of your website. Such buttons tend to be placed statically on the side of the page, like a little Levis tab (albeit one that slides down your jeans when you stand up).

We have such a button on our website. It's a green "Feedback" button on the right-hand side of each page.

Though "Give Feedback" buttons are simple, they can be highly effective, acting as persistent open invitations for feedback.

Tools for "Give Feedback" buttons

You can easily add a "Give Feedback" button using one of the following solutions: Survicate, Feedback Lite, Feedbackify, Usabilla, Qualtrics, Medallia Digital (mobile-friendly), and SurveyGizmo (the "Give Feedback" button is one of its many features). For Conversion Rate Experts' website, for reasons of leanness, we don't use a hosted software solution; we simply link our "Feedback" button to the form on our "Contact Us" page.

The software hosts the feedback forms, and then allows the website's creators to view—and manage—the responses. (In several of the apps, the feedback is managed using an interface similar to that of an email client, having an inbox and folders.) If visitors leave their email addresses, the website's customer-support team can easily reply to the feedback.

Diagnose by…using your website's search tool (to discover what your visitors can't otherwise find)

Your website's "Search This Site" feature is useful in two ways. Not only does it help your visitors find what they are looking for, but the resulting site search report in your analytics package also provides you with a wealth of information about how to improve your website. It tells you what your visitors want but can't find.

Look through the search logs for a particular page.

- Are visitors searching for content that doesn't exist? If so, consider adding it to your website.
- Are they searching for content that does exist? If so, check whether the search would have revealed the most relevant page. Also, consider whether the content they were looking for should be added to—or made more prominent on—the page from which they launched their search.
- What language do the visitors use in their searches? Consider aligning your language with theirs.

Diagnose by...**using search engines** (to be notified when people say things about you)

Search engines allow you to track what the world is saying about your company and products. Moz Fresh Web Explorer is great for this.

Several search engines track mentions in real time, allowing you to discover what people are saying about your website on blogs, forums, and in social media.

As you read through the results, make a list of what people are saying. What do they like about your website? What don't they like about it?

Then consider how you can fix any problems.

When we redesigned our own website, we used this technique to make a list of people who had commented on our old website. We then personally asked those people for feedback about our new design.

Tools for tracking what people are saying about you

The following tools can be useful for tracking mentions: Moz Fresh Web Explorer, Google Alerts, Talkwalker Alerts, Mention, Ninja Outreach, Twitter Search, BuzzSumo, and Facebook.

Salesforce Marketing Cloud provides powerful tools for real-time analysis and monitoring of social media.

Interlude (ice creams not included): why it's essential to empathize with your visitors

The Roman poet Horace once said, "If you wish me to weep, you yourself must first feel grief." In other words, you can't arouse a feeling in someone until you have experienced that feeling yourself.

In his book *Making Ads Pay*, the veteran copywriter John Caples illustrated this by describing a demonstration that his physics professor once carried out (you can see it on YouTube). The professor fastened two tuning forks close to each other, then struck one of them hard with a hammer. Its sound rang out like a chime. Then he seized the vibrating fork with his hand, and the music stopped. To the class's surprise, the other tuning fork had started to vibrate and was giving off the same musical note.

Caples observed that emotional vibrations work in the same way; they travel from one person to another. When you write, the tuning fork within you must vibrate at the same frequency as the tuning forks within your visitors.

So before you can write compelling copy, you must emotionally empathize with your visitors.

It isn't easy, though. As a web marketer, your work is almost intrinsically ivory-tower work. It's hard to even meet your visitors, never mind empathize with them. So how do you develop this emotional resonance?

Quantitative feedback tools—like clickstream analytics—don't help, because they just give you numbers. Qualitative feedback tools—like surveys—can give you the voice of the visitor, but they aren't sufficient to turn you into a tuning fork. Several of the following techniques (method marketing plus to a lesser extent face-to-face selling, encouraging visitors to phone you, and talking to "VOC aggregators")—are what we call *ultra-qualitative*. They are at the core of how we approach conversion. You don't hear much about them because no one has found a way to package them into neat little subscription services. You'll never see ads for them. That doesn't make them any less valuable.

Diagnose by…using method marketing (become a customer so that you understand at least one customer deeply)

Method marketing is a term that was coined by the marketer Denny Hatch. It's inspired by the "method" approach to acting. It's said that when Robert De Niro came to New York for the filming of the movie *Taxi Driver*, he arrived early and proceeded to get a job as a real taxi driver. For two weeks, he worked long shifts. By the time filming began, De Niro was no longer a Hollywood celebrity trying to imagine how it must feel to be a taxi driver. He actually was a taxi driver. He had experienced the dangers. He had suffered the fatigue. And he felt at home in his car. He had gained the *tacit knowledge* of a real taxi driver.

Tacit knowledge is knowledge that is difficult to learn from the words of others. Perhaps the best way to appreciate its power is to read the following list:

Tacit knowledge: things that you can't understand unless you have experienced them

Many things can't be understood unless you've experienced them yourself. People who have had certain experiences find them difficult to articulate to people who haven't:

- being a parent;
- having a migraine;
- orgasm;
- being drunk;

- flying;
- being blind;
- having a loved one die;
- spiritual enlightenment;
- meditation;
- hallucinogens;
- being gay;
- holding your newborn child;
- being underwater;
- the tastes of certain foods;
- being dumped;
- having an addiction;
- having depression, anxiety, stress, or any other type of mental illness;
- being an identical twin; and
- falling in love (incidentally, Norwegians have a word, *Forelsket*, which means "the indescribable euphoria experienced as you begin to fall in love").

In such cases, no amount of explanation can convey the depth of experience. Words aren't enough. You wouldn't understand.

Such hard-to-communicate knowledge is known as *tacit knowledge*. All our consultants gain tacit knowledge by doing method marketing. They become a customer and live the life of the customer. So by the time they begin copywriting, they are writing from the heart. Of course, they then face the challenge of communicating their tacit knowledge, trying to welcome outsiders into the club. That's why copywriting is hard. But at least they are trying to persuade the visitors from the perspective of a knowledgeable insider—not a naive outsider.

As proof of how valuable we think this technique is, the following images show examples of how much commitment we put into it.

To sell Dysons, use Dysons. As part of our research program, we use our clients' products.

Getting under the skin of the customers.

Why are we wearing superhero suits? We helped the company Morphsuits to win an award for fast growth. Morphsuits became the eighteenth fastest growing company in the United Kingdom, and its directors were invited to Richard Branson's house to collect their *Sunday Times* Fast Track awards. The previous photo shows us testing out our fancy dress Morphsuits. It's hard to persuade someone to buy a Lycra bodysuit unless you have personally experienced its benefits ("When you're wearing a Morphsuit, things just happen")—and you have managed to overcome your own objections.

The following photo shows some antibodies that we had ordered from a client that sold scientific supplies. We weren't able to test the antibodies. In fact, we were wary about going anywhere near them. But during the unboxing process, we noticed some valuable information that was wrongly absent from the website.

By following the buying process for these clinical antibodies, we discovered opportunities for growing the client's sales.

If we aren't the target customer, we find someone who is. At this point, marketing becomes anthropology.

To truly understand a product, we become real users. Some products—like this fitness program—require more effort and commitment than others.

You can only truly understand some products—like food supplements—once you have made them part of your life.

There should be no exceptions to this rule. When one of our consultants was uncomfortable joining a dating site to understand how the whole process worked, our cofounder Karl stepped in. Karl stopped short of going on a date, but the process revealed many insights—including the fact that Karl's "datability index" was 40%. (Karl insists that this indicated the presence of a major bug in the website's rating algorithm.)

When growing a company that sold houses, we visited one of the company's sales offices and followed the customer journey of buying a house. (We stopped short of buying the house, a decision we now regret.)

Diagnose by...using method marketing with offline competitors (because the offline world often has solved problems that the online world hasn't)

You can learn a lot from carrying out method marketing with competitors, particularly with offline ones. Most online businesses have offline equivalents that you can visit. Offline companies are less subject to ivory-tower syndrome than online companies, because they have face-to-face contact with customers. Their sales funnels tend to be more sophisticated.

The following photo shows us carrying out grueling research at the local bingo hall:

The onboarding process for offline bingo gave us many ideas for growing an online bingo company.

We learned that offline bingo is excellent regarding usability. Offline bingo halls have solved many problems that online bingo still hadn't solved. New players were led through an elegant onboarding process that introduced them to every type of game and service.

Finally, we have helped to grow several clients in weight loss, including MyFitnessPal, one of the world's most-downloaded mobile apps for weight loss, which recently sold for almost half a billion dollars. And we have learned a lot of techniques by **attending offline weight-loss clubs.**

The great thing about weight-loss groups is that you can speak with real customers. In fact, that's what the meeting is—a one-hour discussion group.

The following photos show Karl starting and finishing a weight-loss program. He adopted the traditional before-and-after poses.

Left: At the first weigh-in, doing the traditional "before" pose. Right: Not so humble now, Karl strutting around like he owns the place, after proudly receiving his Slimmer of the Month award. The activity gave us insights that we have used to grow many clients in the weight-loss industry. (Karl's subsequent fall from grace is not pictured.)

He lost thirty-two pounds and gained even more insights.

Then he regained the pounds.

Diagnose by...becoming a face-to-face salesperson (to learn how to sell the product)

Your website is effectively your 24/7 robot salesperson. And the robot is no smarter than its inventor. If you can't sell your products in person, you'll struggle to sell them online.

Method marketing helps, but it allows you to understand only one customer (yourself). The best way to understand many customers well—albeit not quite so deeply—is to sell the product face-to-face.

In 2003 our founders, Ben and Karl, ran a web business called Mobal that provided cell phones to travelers. Mobal had a large Japanese presence, so Nokia asked Mobal to set up and manage Japan's first bricks-and-mortar Nokia store. We took on the project because we relished the opportunity for our team to spend time selling face-to-face with our visitors.

By opening and running Japan's first Nokia store, we learned rich insights that helped us to triple the sales of an online phone store.

Once the store was open, we created a spreadsheet for our team to complete. It contained two columns:

- **Column 1: Objections.** To this column, our team members added all the objections that they heard from visitors. For example, visitors would say, "Instead of buying one of these phones, I will save money by buying a local prepaid SIM card when I arrive in my destination country."
- **Column 2: Counterobjections.** To this column, our team members added the responses that they found to be the most effective. For example, in response to the objection above, we would reply: "If you buy a local prepaid SIM card at your destination, you won't know

your phone number until you arrive, so your friends and family won't know how to contact you."

The spreadsheet of objections and counterobjections became our knowledge base of tried-and-tested sales copy. We incorporated its content into the website, to great success; we more than doubled the conversion rate and the revenue of the business.

Usually, though, you can't open a bricks-and-mortar store. The following example is from the other end of the scrappiness spectrum. While developing a new type of SIM card for world phones, we realized that we had spent too much time in our office ivory tower. **So we visited a local flea market**, where we spent several hours trying to sell the new prototype product face-to-face.

If you don't have an offline store, create one. Flea markets are an easy way to get in front of users quickly.

At first, we told our stall's visitors that we were carrying out market research and that we wanted to hear their feedback. This had two problems: (1) people didn't want to speak about market research, and (2) those who did tended to give responses that were polite and false. Only when we tried to close the sale did we hear their true objections. So from then on, we tried to sell in earnest (even though our prime motive was to gather feedback). If a visitor showed interest, we would take down their name so we could notify them when the product became available.

This activity became a core part of our process for developing new products. Because our product was aimed at travelers, we soon graduated from flea markets to airports, where we would rent space for an exhibition stand.

Diagnose by...seeing how others describe it in writing (because their words are likely to reveal a lot)

The closer you are to a business, the more you have the "curse of knowledge," the cognitive bias that makes it hard to see things through the eyes of those less experienced. It can help to read how other people have tried to describe your product. The following methods are often useful:

- **Read Wikipedia:** If your company, your product, or the generic type of product has a page on Wikipedia, then study the words that the writers have used. Wikipedia articles are usually excellent in terms of intelligibility, which is particularly important for products that are technical or complex. We have seen several products for which the Wikipedia page was clearer and more persuasive than the company's official landing page. (We once tried, unsuccessfully, to persuade a client to point some of its AdWords traffic at its Wikipedia page.)

- **Read reviews:** Reviews on online stores like Amazon reveal a lot about the buyers' psychology—particularly their likes and dislikes. Pay attention to the wording used in the reviews.

- **Look for places where customers sell the product to others:** There's no purer copywriting than when buyers recommend products to their friends. Search Twitter and Facebook for instances of customers recommending your product to their followers. If your company has a tell-a-friend program that allows the customers to send a personalized message to their friends, then those messages can be a great source of sales copy. (Check first that you are OK to analyze those messages without breaking any laws or terms and conditions.) Not only do the messages reveal the persuasive arguments, but they also tell you the exact wording that customers use. By analyzing the frequency of words used, you can establish the lexicon you should use in your copywriting.

Diagnose by...talking to a "VOC aggregator" (perhaps the fastest way to understand users)

What VOC aggregators are, and why you need to find yours

According to Paul Graham of Y Combinator, to grow an early stage web business, you should spend all of your waking hours on the following three activities:

- Build the product.
- Talk to users.
- Exercise.

We agree. We spend a good fraction of our time talking with our clients' users. It's priceless, but it's also time-consuming.

So we also talk to people who spend their whole lives speaking with users. For example, salespeople, consultants, and customer-support staff. We call these people "Voice-of-Customer Aggregators" (or "VOC aggregators"). VOC aggregators already understand the users. And they don't just know facts like "The average user is forty years old with 2.4 children"; they know the users intuitively, much like you know your own family. In fact, they can often second-guess how the users would react to a particular idea. Plus, because they speak with so many users, they know the relative importance of each issue. When you talk to a VOC aggregator, you harness the wisdom of thousands of hours of conversations with users.

Of course, you still need to talk to users. But you can

accelerate your understanding by identifying your market's VOC aggregators and then talking to them.

With this in mind, the updated formula would be:

- Build the product.
- Talk to users—*and to people who talk to users.*
- Exercise.

How to benefit from VOC aggregation

Here's what you can do:

1. **Identify your own industry's VOC aggregators.** They may be resellers, consultants, telesales people, customer-support people. They may work for your company or for other companies in the same supply chain. They may work for online companies, mail-order companies, or bricks-and-mortar companies. So, for example, when we work for manufacturers of consumer electronics, we spend a lot of time speaking with the staff of bricks-and-mortar electronics stores.
2. **Talk to them.** Ask them how they would sell your product. Their approach is likely to mirror the logic of how their customers buy.
3. **Implement as much of their feedback as you can.** Add the rest to your product road map and marketing road map.

While we were working with Sony, we visited a store that sold its devices. The shop assistant was great at selling the product.

She sold several of the devices each week, and she knew the answers to all the questions that visitors asked. We asked her for her views on the product's website, which she knew well because she had studied it when searching for answers to her visitors' questions. She described twenty-two facts that her visitors needed to know but that weren't mentioned on the company's website. We incorporated these facts into the webpage, making it much more persuasive.

For many products, the salespeople hold decision trees in their heads. What they say depends on how visitors answered the previous questions. In such cases, you should map out the decision trees, consolidate them, and then turn them into conversion flows. We did exactly this for a blue-chip financial services company. After speaking with its call center team, we made changes that resulted in a 214% increase in orders.

Diagnose by…**encouraging your visitors to phone you** (so you can understand them better)

If your phone number is displayed prominently on your pages, speak with your inbound telesales team or whoever answers the calls. They will already understand your visitors deeply, with a level of empathy you could never get from a survey tool. In fact, you may well discover that your page should be a distilled version of words and logic that the salesperson says to the callers.

If the price of your product is low, you may find that it's economically unviable to invite phone calls. Regardless, **we still recommend you add a phone number for just a day or so, for research purposes.** The first few phone calls can reveal breakthrough insights. Not only do phone calls help you to understand your visitors, but they also help you to understand yourself. A phone call can be an "intuition pump"—on the phone, you'll find yourself intuitively using words and logic that you hadn't thought to write on your pages. Just as stand-up comedians come up with many of their best lines while performing in front of an audience, you'll find that much of your best sales copy comes while you are selling on the phone or in person, one-to-one.

Diagnose by...creating—and then studying—a knowledge base of answers to your visitors' questions (to manage the long tail of obstacles)

Knowledge base software helps you to corral users' questions and to organize your responses. By studying the knowledge base, you can understand your visitors' *intentions*, their *likes*, their *objections*, and your most effective *counterobjections*. Plus, the knowledge base doesn't just help you gain insight; it helps visitors to convert.

Tools for knowledge bases

The following knowledge base solutions are popular: Help Scout, Zendesk, KnowledgeOwl, Moxie, Intercom, Helpjuice, and Freshdesk.

Diagnose by...**running user tests** (to see your pages' shortcomings firsthand)

We carry out user tests every day. They are an amazing way to get deep, granular insights into your pages—and to identify exactly how you can make them convert better.

A *user test* (or *usability test*) involves observing someone using your website and noting any issues that arise. User testing is not rocket science—in fact, it's mundane—**but it's perhaps the most powerful technique in this book.**

How to identify your usability problems using usability tests

There are several ways to carry out user tests. Most involve the following:

1. Giving participants tasks to carry out
2. Watching in silence as they complete them
3. Asking them about their thoughts
4. Recording the results for later analysis

How to recruit people to user test your website

Ideally, your participants would be **people who represent**

your target market. However, at first, you can get great results by testing on **whoever's at hand**. Those people sitting near you right now—they'll do. Or a family member. This practice has a name: *hallway usability testing*—which makes it sound more legitimate than it feels when you're doing it. Hallway usability tests are effective because many usability problems are so obvious they could be detected by anyone.

Once you sense that you're getting diminishing returns from your hallway antics, and your website's remaining problems are too sophisticated to be detected by a layman, start to look for test participants who are **from the website's target demographic**. For example, when we doubled the sales of a web app for photographers, we recruited photographers to test the website. You can **recruit visitors directly from the website** using an invitation powered by Ethnio or Hotjar.

It can be surprisingly effective to carry out what we call *retrospective moderated user tests*, in which you contact **someone who has just completed your website's goal** (e.g., made a purchase), and ask them if they'd be willing to retrace their steps. Such people are, by definition, qualified, and have recently gone through all of the thought processes required to buy. Take notes as they show you the path they took through your funnel, and ask them to describe what they thought at each stage. They tend to be excellent at recalling the hoops they had to jump through and the obstacles at which they nearly fell.

Counterintuitively, regardless of which of the previous methods you choose for recruiting, you tend to learn more from **users who *aren't* web-savvy**. People who use the web a lot tend to be better at coping with pages that contain errors. People who don't use the web much are more easily derailed—and can therefore provide more insights.

How to carry out a user test

If the participants aren't from your exact target market, tell them **anything they need to imagine:**

- **Do they need to pretend they are someone else?** For example, if you were working on the website of a car manufacturer, you might say to the test participant, "Imagine that you owned a car made by [company]."
- **Do they need to pretend they are in a particular situation?** For example, you may need to say, "Imagine that you are an existing customer and your car has broken down."

Then, **give them the task** you'd like them to complete. The task is usually a typical goal of the website. For example, if your website sells quirky gifts, the task might be "Add to your basket some smoking mittens, some metal-detecting sandals, and a photo-realistic bacon scarf" (those are all real products, amazingly). You may choose to set the goal in general terms or specifically, depending on whether you want to exclude certain possibilities:

- To consider all possibilities, you may **state the goal implicitly**: "Imagine that your car has broken down. What would you do next?" (About ten years ago, we carried out a user test in which the participant, to our surprise, asked for a Yellow Pages, and didn't even consider using a computer.)
- To be more specific, you may choose to **state the goal in general terms**: "How would you get your car repaired?"
- You may choose to **state the goal specifically**: "Assume you have typed [search terms] into Google and clicked on the first search result. You arrive on this page. How would you find the location of your nearest repair center?"

Encourage criticism. The participant needs to know that you won't take criticism personally. We sometimes find it helps to pretend that the website was designed by someone else, and that we aren't happy with it. That way, the user feels more comfortable criticizing it.

You want the visit to be as natural as possible. Tell them that once they have started the task, you'll stay quiet and watch, and you'll refrain from helping unless they really need you.

During the test, take notes. You'll soon have a huge list of ideas for improving your website. Most tests provide something worthwhile, and it's rare to go more than three tests without getting an idea that's so important you'll want to stop everything until it's implemented.

Steve Krug, the author of a great book called *Don't Make Me Think*, has a useful script (a Word document) for carrying out user tests. The script was designed for user tests in labs, so you may want to ignore the references to microphones and screen recordings.

The hardest thing about user testing is the emotional aspect. Not only can they feel awkward, but also they can make you want to cry. Because the truth hurts. For that reason, most marketers shy away from them. The best marketers are those who rapidly accept the criticism, use it to improve the page, and then user test again.

How to outsource your user testing

If you are too busy—or introverted—to carry out usability tests, you can pay for a service to do *unmoderated user tests* for you. Here's how the services typically work:

- You tell the service which page you want to test.
- You select the type of users that you'd like to participate.
- You specify what the user's task should be.
- After a delay, usually of a few hours, you will receive videos of users carrying out the task.

The following services provide unmoderated user tests:

- UserTesting, WhatUsersDo, TryMyUI (mobile-friendly), Userlytics, UserBob, and Userbrain.
- Lookback (mobile-friendly) is similar, but you provide

the participants (you might choose to send your existing customers to it).

- UsersThink and userinput are low-cost alternatives that provide written reports instead of videos.
- UsabilityHub allows you to carry out tests for free, provided that, in exchange, you complete other people's tests.
- Watchsend is for iPhone apps.
- Testapic provides a user testing service in French; uxline does it in Spanish; Testaisso does it in Portuguese.

To learn more about usability testing, see our talk, "How to make millions from usability testing."

Tools for recording the screen during user tests

You can use one of the following to record your screen during a user test: Camtasia, ScreenFlow, Jing, Morae, Silverback, and UX Recorder (for iOS websites). Some of those tools can also simultaneously record video from the webcam, so you can capture the users' facial expressions (frustration, confusion, despondency, etc.).

How to identify usability problems caused by technical errors

One type of usability problem occurs when the website malfunctions. This is particularly common when the visitor is using an uncommon device or browser version—or when the page is new. The solution is to follow a robust quality-assurance process before any page goes live. *Smashing Magazine*'s list of "45 web design checklists and questionnaires" can be useful.

Session-recording software can help a lot with finding such problems. Options include Clicktale, Inspectlet, Hotjar, and Tealeaf—all of which also help to identify problems with online forms.

Other tools and services for user testing

You might also want to check out the following tools for user testing:

- Loop11, UsabilityHub, and UserZoom are useful.
- Mechanical Turk can be used to find participants.
- Pear Note and Reframer help you to write notes while observing a user test.
- If you are a usability expert, Capian can help you to create reports of your expert reviews.
- The Accessibility Priority Tool is a spreadsheet that scores different aspects of a website's usability and accessibility.

There's a great benefit in carrying out at least a few user tests yourself

Whichever tools and services you use, we highly recommend that you (and everyone else who creates pages for your website) should carry out at least a few tests. By testing in-person, you can ask questions of the users. You can even propose solutions to their objections, and collaborate with them on the solutions.

We talk more about user testing in an article called "How to eliminate the usability problems that stifle your growth," which you can find on our website.

Diagnose by...**using eye tracking** (to identify where your visitors are looking)

Just because something is on your page doesn't mean that anyone looks at it. While your users are participating in user tests, you can track their eye movements using an eye-tracking apparatus.

Users' gaze is influenced by surrounding cues. For example, they tend to look at whatever the person on the page is looking at. (Image credit: Objective and Tobii.)

Eye tracking is great for understanding how users look at webpages. The data from a browsing session can be converted into a movie of the user's eye movements, or displayed as a static chart like a heat map or movement map.

Professional eye-tracking hardware tends to cost thousands of dollars. However, a service called LookTracker allows you to get professional eye-tracking reports on demand. The LookTracker service works much like the user testing tools mentioned above. EyesDecide provides a similar service, but the eye-tracking reports are gathered via the users' webcams.

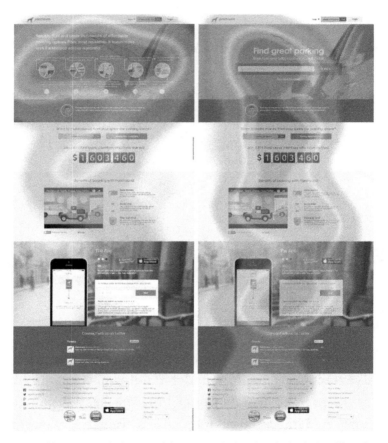

Eye tracking can reveal what your visitors see and what they don't. The headline of the right-hand page is more compelling, causing visitors to read on. (Image credit: EyesDecide.)

EyeQuant and Feng-GUI use a computer algorithm to predict your visitors' eye tracking, based on the contrast and layout of the page elements.

Diagnose by...**using pop-up surveys** (to recruit participants for your user tests)

Once you have fixed the more obvious problems with your website, it's time to carry out some user tests on *qualified* prospects—that is, people who actually visit your website.

A software platform called Ethnio provides an easy way of recruiting people for user tests. In this chapter, we'll describe its features. Hotjar (mobile-friendly) has this feature too, and you could probably create the same functionality using a combination of other tools.

Once Ethnio is installed on your website, you can use it to easily display a pop-up survey that asks your visitors if they'd like to participate in a user test. You can target the survey to specific types of visitors—for example, those who use a particular browser or are in a specific geolocation. You can design the survey to ask questions that will help you to determine whether you want to interview the person. For example, you may ask them why they visited your site and whether this is their first visit.

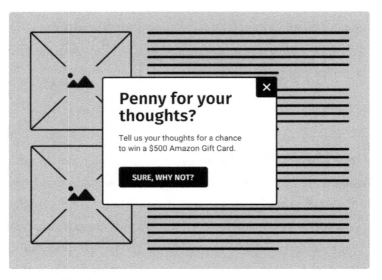

A overlay inviting users to participate in a user test.

To incentivize people for participating in your tests, you'll probably need to offer a reward. We like to reward people with gift cards from Amazon.com, because they are quick to send and they require only the recipient's email address. Also, visitors instantly recognize them as being valuable— they're clearly not some sneaky voucher that's full of weasel clauses and restrictions. With an incentive, about 5% of visitors tend to respond, though this varies greatly from industry to industry.

People's willingness to participate in user tests depends on which type of market you're in; visitors to some types of website—such as financial services or health issues—tend to be reluctant to start a conversation. In other markets, visitors love to get involved.

Once visitors have completed the survey, their details

appear in a table in Ethnio's or Hotjar's interface. You can then decide whether you'd like to carry out a user test with them.

Ethnio's control panel allows you to manage your user tests. (Image credit: Ethnio.)

You can interview them however you like—by phone (with screen-sharing software such as join.me, Zoom, GoToMeeting) or in person. Ethnio can also help you to set up the call.

Bear in mind that the people who want to be interviewed are self-selecting; they don't necessarily represent your average visitor. In particular, they may be more time-rich and cash-poor than your average visitor. However, they still tend to be much more qualified than your average user testing participant.

It can help to record the phone call. To do so, you'll need to get the user's permission.

Ethnio provides a great sample script to use when interviewing visitors.

Measure your wins...**using A/B testing** (to test different versions of your webpages to see which is the best)

A/B testing software allows you to create different variations of a page and then measure which converts best. You can then promote the winning page to become your official new version.

A/B testing doesn't generate many insights. However, it does give the final word on whether your insights and intuitions were accurate. A winning A/B test is your visitors voting with their feet (and often their credit cards).

For further information on A/B testing, see a report we wrote titled "A/B testing 101." Also, we recommend you read the help files for whatever A/B testing software you use. The help files tend to be written well, and their advice will be correct for that software and whichever methods and algorithms it uses.

Tools for A/B testing

Popular platforms include Optimizely, Google Optimize, VWO, Convert.com, and Adobe Target. There are many alternatives, though. We created the industry's first and most comprehensive comparison website for them. It compares software solutions for split-testing—A/B testing and multivariate testing—allowing you to see the differences easily.

Unsure which software to use for A/B-testing?

Here's the ultimate comparison of A/B testing software, multivariate testing tools and split-testing platforms.

Hover over the table headings to learn more.

	Initial set-up cost	Ongoing costs	Technology compatibility	A/B or MVT?	Type of MVT	Can it be self hosted	Can multiple goals be set?	Can traffic be segmented?	Used on email campaigns	Has a platform for creating webpages
TASTY AB Tasty	Free Trial	From €40	Client-side	Both	Full factorial	✔	✔	✔	✔	✔
accenture Accenture Omni-Channel Testing Platform	~$33,000	$160,000–$320,000	Client-side	Both	Several (see details)	✔	✔	✔	✔ (see details)	✗
Adobe Adobe Target	Contact Adobe	Usually a four-figure monthly fee	Server-side	Both	Taguchi	✔ (see details)	✔	✔	✔	✗
OPENTEXT OpenText Optimost	Contact OpenText Optimost	Usually a four-figure monthly fee	Client-side	Both	Optimal design	✗	✔	✔	✔	✗
ClickThroo ClickThroo	None	$195–$1195 /month	Server-side	A/B	N/A	✗	✔	✔	✔	✔
	Contact	Monthly fee	Client-side	Both	Full factorial	Contact	✔	✔	✔	✗

Our comprehensive summary of A/B testing tools:
www.conversion-rate-experts.com/split-testing-software/

How to measure what's working if your website doesn't get much traffic

In the chapter on low-traffic websites, we explained how it can be difficult to measure what's working on low-traffic websites, because A/B tests often don't reach significance.

Many people with low traffic websites thus believe that testing isn't suitable for them.

But that isn't the case. Done correctly, there's no reason why you shouldn't be testing often on your website and realizing all the benefits that go with it.

How many conversions do you need for A/B testing? It depends on the following factors:

- **Your current conversion rate.** The fewer conversions you get, the longer it takes to detect a doubling.
- **The increase in conversion rate that you're trying to detect.** A 100% increase can be detected about four times as fast as a 50% increase.
- **How statistically confident you want to be.** If you wanted to be 99.99% sure that your new page wasn't winning just by chance, you'd have to wait a long time.

So what should a low-traffic website do? Several strategies are effective:

- **Test the biggest, boldest ideas.** When you have low traffic, it's especially important to test big, bold ideas that are more likely to move the needle significantly. Test things that your visitors care about. Overcome their main objections. Highlight the things they love. Change the offer, or at least how it's presented. Test things that might double or halve the number of conversions, but are unlikely to make no difference.
- **Measure "micro-conversions."** Imagine conversion goals as a spectrum. On the right-hand side of the spectrum is what you ideally want—something like net profit or lifetime customer value. Such metrics tend to be untimely, meaning that you'd take months or years to measure their true value. On the left-hand side of the spectrum lie metrics like click-through rate or engagement rate. Such "intermediate" metrics are much larger

in number and can be measured instantly, but you can't be confident that they correlate with overall long-term success. The less traffic your website gets, the more you need to rely on "intermediate" metrics toward the left-hand side of the spectrum.

- **Test on major pages.** Maybe this one is obvious, but test only those pages that almost all of your customers see, like your main landing page or your checkout funnel.

- **Combine similar pages into one test.** If you have ten landing pages, and you want to test the call-to-action button, then apply the same change to all of those pages and include them in the same test. Some companies have many more landing pages than they need, maybe because they wanted to make each landing page bespoke to a particular keyword. We often consolidate such pages into one, and then optimize the heck out it.

- **Reduce the statistical significance at which you'll declare a winner.** It has become the norm to declare a winning test at a statistical significance of 95%, but that's not to say you can't use a different figure. It would be a shame to conclude that "If I can't have 95% confidence, I won't run an A/B test at all." That's like saying, "I'm a perfectionist. If I can't do it perfectly, I won't do it at all." Most marketing decisions are made without any measurement, so don't rule out the possibility of ending a test at, say, 90% confidence—or even 85% confidence—especially if the alternative is just to launch the page and hope for the best. Sure, your chances of declaring false positives increase slightly, but the benefits of being able to test more ideas usually hugely outweighs the slim risk of promoting a page that was actually losing.

- **Fixed-period testing.** Many A/B testing tools now monitor your tests on an ongoing basis and tell you when there's a winner. In addition, though, you may choose to specify a maximum duration for each test, after which you'll make a decision regardless. If the control was winning at that point, you may choose to promote it. If the challenger was winning, and you're confident that it was based on a research-driven hypothesis, then you may choose to promote it. If the challenger was based on a risky hypothesis, you may choose not to take the risk. Either way, this approach is more rigorous than how most early stage companies make decisions.
- **Temporarily increase the amount of traffic to the page being tested**, even if it means sacrificing some profitability. If the new page wins, the traffic may turn out to be more profitable than you had expected.

You can estimate how long an A/B test would take by using a calculator like Optimizely's.

Regardless of whether you carry out A/B tests, we *highly* recommend you use user tests as a way of measuring the performance of pages. In fact, if the A/B test duration calculator shows that your all of your tests would take more than six months, we recommend you use *only* user tests, and return to A/B testing once your business has grown.

User tests have many, huge advantages over A/B tests:

- **They are quick to carry out.** A user test can take less than ten minutes.
- They allow you to gather **qualitative insights**. A two-month-long A/B test may tell you which page performed better, but a ten-minute-long user test tells you why.
- They provide insights that are **granular.** An A/B test will only reveal which page is better—that's just one fact about the whole page—but a user test will reveal which parts of the page work.

Know your market by...**analyzing your competitors** (to see what they have learned about their visitors)

Although it's not our favorite technique, it can be useful to analyze the websites of your competitors, for two reasons:

1. You may find that they have recognized—and solved—a problem that you haven't.
2. You need to work out how you will position your company relative to your competitors. After all, your visitors will be looking at your competitors' websites too. No company exists in a vacuum.

You may wish to also **carry out user tests on your compet-**

itors' websites, to get an independent view on how users perceive them.

You can learn a lot from your competitors. But to beat them, you'll need to do things they don't.

Why each of the twenty-five techniques for understanding your visitors is like a spotlight

Now that you know what each of the twenty-five techniques does, try to identify which combination of them will give you the insights you need.

As in many fields of creativity, it helps to have a spirit of experimentation. Don't give up because your first attempt did not reveal insights. Each technique and each question is like a spotlight that shines light on a different aspect of your visitors' behavior. The more information you gather, the more problems and opportunities you will spot.

You might, for example, discover that your visitors' main objection is that they don't trust you. Or that you don't provide what they want. Or that they like what they see, but they are just browsing.

How do you remedy those problems?

You look them up in Section 3, that's how...

Making websites win

The most common problems that make web visitors abandon—and proven, easy-to-implement solutions

The **ingredients** of a winning website

At the end of Section 1, we described the DiPS (Diagnose → Problem → Solution) formula for improving websites.

We explained how you need to begin with *diagnosis*, to identify how your website can be improved.

Then, in Section 2, we described twenty-five diagnosis techniques we use. After implementing just a few of them, you'll have a big list of identified *problems* (which you may prefer to think of as *opportunities*).

This section is about implementing *solutions* to those problems (opportunities). A good solution is one that eliminates the problem entirely, unblocking your website's profits like that gloopy stuff unblocks the hairs from a shower drain—and in a manner that's no less satisfying.

Fortunately, not all blockages are unique. During the hundreds of research projects we have carried out, we have identified the major categories into which most problems fall. Your company's biggest problem will almost certainly be among them. Each of the following chapters is dedicated to one of those problems. Some of them are subtle; if you miss them, or fail to recognize their scope, you could waste time working on the wrong aspect of your business. (We see this happen a lot.) By reading each chapter, you'll become better at spotting each problem when you see it in research data.

Here's how to use this section of the book: Refer to your research to identify which problem is causing your visitors to abandon your website. Then, skip to the corresponding chapter, which will explain how to think about the problem, and will then describe some proven, effective ways of fixing it. Of course, there are many way to overcome each problem. For example, there are over a hundred ways of overcoming lack of trust, and some of them are much more effective than others. For each problem, we will describe strategies that we've found to be robust—that tend to work reliably in most situations.

Winning websites…are written well: if visitors can't understand your writing, here's how to improve it

Why you should learn to write clearly—and why so few people are good at it

When we ask a website's visitors why they didn't buy, they often report that they were confused. They hadn't understood the words on the site. And visitors can't buy what they can't understand.

So, with millions of dollars at stake, why are many websites confusing?

Because writing intelligibly is harder than it sounds. For example, read the following sentence from a popular newspaper, written by an otherwise great writer:

> Dance music aficionados can argue interminably over which of the legendary singles Frankie Knuckles produced in the late 80s—singles, you can say without fear of contradiction, that played a part in changing the face of pop music for ever—is the best.

That sentence is free of typos and punctuation errors. And it uses sophisticated words accurately. According to many rules of English, it's written well.

Yet most people struggle to understand it, let alone work out what's wrong with it, or how to fix it.

It's hard to write clearly. In fact, it's hard to find someone who can teach you how to write clearly. Schools tend to spend more time teaching pupils how to sound smart, or how to analyze Shakespearian prose, than how to be understood. Students are more likely to be told to memorize poetry than to carry out a readability test.

This is a disservice. Poetry can be life-enriching, but the purpose of almost all writing is to communicate information.

So if your school didn't teach you how to write intelligibly, how can you learn?

This chapter describes some fantastic resources for helping you to write more clearly. They have helped us to generate hundreds of millions for our clients. It's hard to overstate how useful they are.

But first, let's explore why so many writers are hard to understand.

Many books teach you to avoid errors, but that's not the problem

When most people want to improve their writing, they buy a book like *"Eats, Shoots & Leaves: The Zero Tolerance Approach to Punctuation,"* which is about how to avoid making mistakes. Such books describe rules like the following:

- "When there are parentheses at the end of a sentence, put the period after the closing parenthesis (like this)."
- "If your whole sentence is in parentheses, put the period *inside* the closing parenthesis. (Like this.)"

Such rules may be useful to know, but they make little difference to whether your readers understand what you are saying.

Many teachers specialize in sounding intelligent; if you follow their advice, your sales will plummet

Many teachers encourage writing in what Richard Lanham calls the "Official Style"—a style that sounds intelligent but that is hard to read. Lanham's book *Revising Prose* teaches you how to translate Official-Style sentences into plain language. It contains a great example of how Warren Buffett, the world's most-famous investor, translated a fund prospectus into plain language. Buffett changed hard-to-read sentences like

> "Adjustments made to shorten portfolio maturity and duration are made to limit capital losses during periods when interest rates are expected to rise"

into easy-to-read text:

> "When we expect a major and sustained increase in rates, we will concentrate on short-term issues."

No wonder fellow investors hang on Buffett's every word.

The Official Style is prevalent in academic literature too. On the website LOL My Thesis, graduates self-deprecatingly translate the titles of their theses from the Official Style into plain language—usually to comic effect:

- **Original title of thesis:** "Environmental enrichment and the striatum: The influence of environment on inhibitory circuitry within the striatum of environmentally enriched animals and behavioural consequences." **Rewritten title:** "Having toys and bright colours in their cages makes mice smarter in their brains!"
- **Original title of thesis:** "Challenging ritual and exploring deposition within the canals of Chavín de Huántar." **Rewritten title:** "Ancient Peruvians threw stuff down a drain: maybe it was ritual, probably just trash."
- **Original title of thesis:** "The Punch Brothers' The Blind Leaving the Blind: how heterogeneous stylistic techniques provide new interpretations of genre." **Rewritten title:** "A band that detests genre classifications is just gonna have to put up with it."

The rewritten titles are facetious, and many of them omit useful information. But they also reveal a truth: The Official Style is like medieval armor. It defends you from attack, but people can no longer hear what you're saying.

If you were to write your website in the Official Style, your conversion rate would bomb. Your visitors would leave confused. Teachers and bosses may like intelligent-sounding text, but readers prefer text that's easy to understand.

How to write so that people will understand you

Faced with all this bad advice, how can you learn to write well? Clear writing is a big subject for a little chapter, so in this chapter we describe several tools and techniques that will help immensely—and then we recommend some resources that will transform your life with just a few hours' effort.

A simple technique that helps you to write easy-to-read copy

By far the most effective technique for improving your writing is simple: carry out readability tests. A readability test is simply a user test carried out specifically on a piece of writing.

If you run readability tests on everything you write, you'll quickly become aware of how your readers struggle. Make a note of every point at which they falter, and then fix it. You can make the fixes during the test, or afterward, depending on how much fixing there is to do, and how quick you are at editing.

Speak first, write later

If you struggle to write clearly, you will find the following workaround useful. One of our clients, a company called Moz, had a common problem. Moz's founder, Rand Fishkin, mentioned that in seven minutes he could persuade almost anyone to sign up. So face-to-face, Rand's conversion rate was high. But he was frustrated that his website's conversion rate was much lower.

We asked Rand to film himself saying what he would say during those seven minutes.

Rand Fishkin was masterful at selling his company's service face-to-face—so we recorded him doing it.

We transcribed the video, then used the transcript as a template for the company's new landing page. And we embedded the video itself into the page.

The new page beat the old one, with a 52% higher conversion rate during the A/B test. Rand reported that, in total, we almost tripled his company's conversion rate. (If you'd like to learn more about this project, see the detailed case study we wrote about it.)

Many people find that their spoken English is easier to

understand than their written English. If you are one of those people, try the following workflow:

- Record yourself.
- Get the recording transcribed. We highly recommend Speechpad for fast, accurate transcription.
- Edit your transcript and incorporate it into your website.
- A/B test the new page to confirm that your changes have increased your profits.

Be aware of the reader's memory buffer

To make your writing easy to understand, there's one principle above all others that you should understand: You should be constantly aware of the reader's *memory buffer*. As a person reads, his or her brain constantly processes and interprets the incoming words. In doing so, it loads the words into a short-term memory—a buffer—and then discharges them when the meaning has been understood.

The buffer memory is surprisingly small—it struggles to hold more than about fifteen words. Fortunately, most sentences contain frequent resolution points, at which the meaning can be understood and the buffer unloaded. In the following examples, we have labeled with pipes ("|") the main resolution points—the points at which the words in the buffer can be interpreted. We have also labeled, in everfading shades, the points at which the short-term memory has gone too long without a break.

Dance music aficionados| can argue interminably over| which of the legendary singles Frankie Knuckles produced in the late 80s— singles, you can say without fear of contradiction, that played a part in changing the face of pop music for ever—is the best.|

The pipes feel like points at which your brain gets to "take a breath." When you read the faded words, you may get the same panicky feeling that you get when you are diving underwater and you are starting to run out of oxygen. By the time you reach the final pipe, your short-term memory is gasping for breath.

The following text contains another example of the same phenomenon:

To pass the Bechdel test,| a movie must have at least two female characters| who are named| and talk to each other| about something other than a man.|

Pulp Fiction, all three movies of the original *Star Wars* trilogy, *Harry Potter and the Deathly Hallows: Part II*, *The Social Network*, *Avatar,* and *Finding Nemo* reportedly fail the test.|

To understand where those resolution points (the pipes) lie, you could study linguistic parse trees. However, they are hard to learn. Fortunately, there's an easier way. With a few minutes' practice, you'll discover that you can sense it, just by reading a sentence word by word, and noting the points at which your understanding resolves.

(Incidentally, *dependency length* is the number of words during which the reader needs to "hold their breath" before they can reach a resolution point.)

If you aim to go easy on your readers' memory buffers, several priceless rules of thumb emerge:

- You can enforce resolution points by **keeping sentences short.** A period is a resolution point. As you become more sophisticated, you'll discover that certain types of long sentences are fine, provided they have what's called right-branched clauses, like this one, or this one, or even this one.
- In each sentence, **minimize the distance between the start of the subject and the end of the verb.** In the example above, we mentioned the following sentence: "*Pulp Fiction*, all three movies of the original *Star Wars* trilogy, *Harry Potter and the Deathly Hallows: Part II*, *The Social Network*, *Avatar*, and *Finding Nemo* reportedly fail the test." You could improve it by moving the verb *fail* to the start: "The following movies reportedly fail the test: The original *Star Wars* trilogy, *Harry Potter and the Deathly Hallows: Part II*, *Pulp Fiction*, *The Social Network*, *Avatar*, and *Finding Nemo*."
- **"Omit needless words,"** advised Strunk and White. Buffer memory is the reason. Needless words don't just waste time; they make ideas too big to fit in buffer memories.
- **Replace nominalizations with action verbs.** Nomi-

nalizations are where verbs are stated as though they were nouns. So, for example,

- *Meet* becomes *a meeting.*
- *Investigated* becomes *an investigation.*
- *Tested* becomes *a test.*

Nominalizations are bad because they require a (usually meaningless) verb, like *had*, plus prepositions to link them:

- *Meet* becomes *had a meeting.* (What was being *had?*)
- *Investigated* becomes *held an investigation.* (What was being *held?*)
- *Tested* becomes *carried out a test.* (What was *carried?*)

You can spot nominalizations by looking for verbs that aren't really describing what's happening (like *had*, *held*, and *carried* in the sentences above). The verb *to be* is the most common culprit. If you ever see *to be* (or its variations like *is* and *was*), you'll probably find a more action-ey verb hiding nearby, maybe inside a noun. Ask yourself, what is actually being done here? For example, when you see the following sentence:

My recommendation *is* to carry out an improvement initiative on the website

the word *is* indicates that the verb is hiding elsewhere. In this case, it's in the word *improvement*. You should rewrite the sentence as follows:

I recommend we improve the website.

If in doubt, use the following sentence structure

The human brain is great at understanding sentences that have the following structure:

The woman threw the ball to the dog.

In other words...

A living entity does something (maybe to something else, preferably another living entity).

Next time you are struggling to write a sentence, try writing it in that format. For most conversion copywriting, the living entities should be *you* (the reader) and *we* (the company).

When you first try it, you'll feel like it isn't going to work. You'll be surprised how often it does.

A few more tips for writing good sentences

The following tips can improve any sentence:

· **Make abstract sentences concrete.** Ask yourself, "If

I were making a movie of this sentence, what would I point the camera at?" And then describe that.
- **Use action verbs,** verbs that describe what is actually happening.
- You'd always put the punchline at the end of a joke. Similarly, **put the main point of a sentence at its end.** To check that you've done this right, read the sentence out loud and hammer your fist on the desk to emphasize the the last word(s). If the words are in the wrong order, the hammering will sound silly.

  - **Bad:** The hammer test reveals that the words are in a suboptimal order *in this sentence.*
  - **Good:** This sentence has its words in a better order, and so *the hammer test works great.*

- If you ever find yourself italicizing or bolding a word to add emphasis, that's a clue that the word might belong at the end of the sentence. Rearrange the sentence to put the word at the end, and see if it sounds better that way.

Hemingway "makes your writing bold and clear"

Hemingway highlights long, complex sentences and common errors. It's free. You won't agree with all of its suggestions, but it provides a fresh pair of (robot) eyes. We use it regularly.

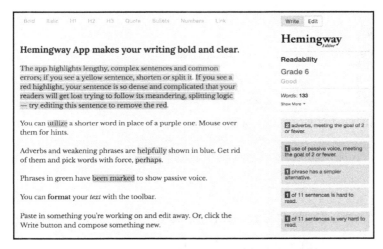

The Hemingway app suggests how you could have made your sentences easier to read.

Grammarly: "The world's most accurate grammar checker"

Grammarly is the best proofreading tool we've found. Like Hemingway, it isn't always right, but it can point out mistakes that you have overlooked.

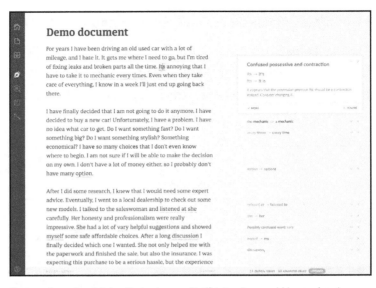

Grammarly spots mistakes that even your English teacher would have missed.

Some fantastic resources to improve your writing

On our office bookshelf, we have fifty-two books about writing, but only a few of them will help you to improve the *clarity* of your writing.

We recommend you start at the top of the following list and work your way down. If punctuation bores you, don't be deterred. **Most of the books aren't about grammatical pedantry**; they are about simple, practical techniques that will transform you into a better writer. The one by Stephen Wilbers is so good—so *transformational*—you'll be amazed you haven't discovered it before.

- **Free guides from the Plain English Campaign.** The

Plain English Campaign has some useful free guides. Start with "How to write in plain English." Then read "The A to Z of alternative words," which urges you to use words like *use* instead of utilizing words like *utilize*.

- The second half of **The Elements of Style by Strunk and White** (the section written by E.B. White) concisely describes how to write clearly—and why it's important to do so.

- The first 86 pages of **A Pocket Style Manual by Diana Hacker and Nancy Sommers** include all the grammar and punctuation advice you'll ever need (explained extremely concisely), plus many tips for making your writing readable. **This is the only book that we keep on our desks.**

- *Keys to Great Writing* **by Stephen Wilbers. This is our favorite book on the list.** It teaches you the mechanics of writing well. It's brilliantly concise and is full of techniques that actually work. You have probably never heard of most of them. You may enjoy this book even if you hated English classes at school. We suspect that it particularly appeals to programmers, because it provides a much-needed logical framework for writing. The book summarizes several other books, including two other favorites of ours: *Style: The Basics of Clarity and Grace* and *The Sense of Structure: Writing from the Reader's Perspective.*

- *Writing Tools: 55 Essential Strategies for Every Writer* **by Roy Peter Clark.** Why have we begun this paragraph with a question that we immediately answer? Because that's a useful literary technique for introducing a subject. If you'd like to discover more literary techniques, this book is full of them. Once you become aware of each technique, you'll begin to spot it in other people's writing.

- *The Sense of Style* by **Steven Pinker.** Pinker is a cognitive scientist. In this book he explains how a knowledge of linguistics can help you to write better. By teaching you how language works, he helps you to become more intuitive about how to write well. If you want an even deeper understanding of how language works, then read Pinker's prior book *The Language Instinct*.

- *The Elements of Eloquence* by **Mark Forsyth.** This book describes simple techniques that help you to write great phrases. The techniques appear in almost all great writing (particularly poetry, song lyrics, and marketing slogans). This is one of those books that makes you wonder, "How come they resisted teaching me that at school? Did my teachers not know all those awesome techniques—but Shakespeare, Bob Dylan, and Paul Simon did?" Unlike some books about writing, this one works great as an audiobook.

Every chapter in this section is, to some extent, about writing—what to say, how to say it, and when to say it. However, it all begins with writing clearly. That's a prerequisite to everything else.

If you write intelligibly, you stand a chance of persuading your visitors.

And if you don't, you don't.

Winning websites...are user-friendly: if visitors struggle to use your website, here's how to make it easy to use

Usability problems kill conversions.

There's no easier way to grow a business than to eliminate them.

We have described how user tests can help you to identify usability problems. In this chapter, we describe how to solve them.

Why are so many designers "usability blind"?

If you're a sadist with a technical bent, you will enjoy running usability tests. During tests, we see users caught in wild-goose chases, scratching their heads, and sometimes swearing or even hitting their keyboards.

Why do marketers make websites that cause people to punch peripherals? Because marketers are afflicted with the *curse of knowledge*, a cognitive bias that makes it extremely difficult to think about a problem from the perspective of someone who's less informed. Marketers spend so long looking at their own websites, they can't imagine what it would be like to see the website for the first time.

As a result, the website's users appear to be stupid. It's a compelling illusion. But look at it another way:

1. Our users desired something.
2. We created a website to satisfy that desire.
3. And our users still can't get what they desire.

Now who's stupid?

How can you overcome the curse of knowledge? Design your processes for what you perceive to be a busy, lazy, drunk, amnesiac idiot—what lawyers call a "moron in a hurry" (really). Even geniuses with time on their hands will be grateful that you did.

Why is usability hard to learn?

Usability is hard to learn because great examples are hard to detect. Usable solutions are invisibly elegant—like you never notice that you have a spleen until you have a problem with your spleen.

Also, for reasons we don't understand, some people seem to be almost genetically predisposed to recognizing usability. And others seem to be blind to it.

How can you design pages that are easy to use?

It can take years to become great at designing easy-to-use pages. The following tips can help a lot:

1. Watch a lot of user tests

Most people are surprised when they first watch a user test. They are surprised that the visitors see and do things they hadn't expected. The more you watch user tests, the more you internalize the insights and become empathetic. First, you become aware how of how erratic users can be. After that, you become better at second-guessing how users will behave.

2. Watch eye-tracking sessions

Eyes don't move the way one might expect. They move from fixation point to fixation point in rapid jumps called *saccades*. The more you watch eye-tracking sessions, the more you become aware of how users see (and don't see) things. You learn the importance of controlling the users' eye movements.

3. Learn all the user-interface elements that are at your disposal

As you use the web, become aware of the page elements that each website uses. The best conversion practitioners have an almost encyclopedic knowledge of the web. They appear to have read the whole of the internet. It comes in useful. When faced with a particular problem, it helps to be able to recall how another website has effectively solved it. We are avid collectors of effective marketing elements. Every time you see something that works well, take a screenshot of it and store it in a "swipe file" folder. Incidentally, this doesn't just apply to the web. Our swipe file contains thousands of examples from direct mail and offline space advertising for almost every industry.

4. Learn the most important concepts of usability

There are many good books about usability, but the following ones will teach you most of the concepts you need to know:

- *Don't Make Me Think* by **Steve Krug** is an excellent introduction to web usability. We passionately believe it should be on the school curriculum.
- *Designed for Use* by **Lukas Mathis** is less entertaining than *Don't Make Me Think*, but it covers more usability concepts. If this book list seems worryingly short, that's testament to how much ground this book covers.
- *The Visual Display of Quantitative Information* by **Edward R. Tufte** contains many examples of complex data shown in beautifully elegant ways. Don't be put off by its technical-sounding title. It's fun to read.

5. Use tools for wireframing and prototyping (so your designs can be user tested before they get coded up)

To make your designs usable, design them in a format that makes them easy to edit. (In fact, that's true for anything you ever create.) Once you have designed a first draft, user test it on one or two people, and then incorporate your insights into the design and user test again.

In doing so, you get a frequent sanity check that you are proceeding along the right lines.

Every medium has its own low-fidelity format.

Fiction writers use plot outlines. Moviemakers use storyboards. Artists use pencil outlines. And web designers use wireframes.

A wireframe shows the layout of a page, with key text, but without any detail. Most of the images in Section 3 of this book are wireframes. The most important feature of a wireframe (or of any low-fidelity format) is that it contains only the core ideas with no incidental trimmings. This gives three big advantages:

1. Wireframes are easy to create and edit. A change that takes a company a week to implement on a live website may take ten seconds to make on a wireframe.
2. Wireframes are easy to interpret. We once observed a user test of a page that had been designed in high fidelity. "I don't like the colors," the user commented. "Ignore the colors," the designer replied. "I don't like the cartoon dog," the user said. "Ignore the dog," the designer replied. "I don't like the feel of the page," the user said. "Ignore the feel," the designer responded. The user became irritated: "For heaven's sake, what are you asking me to look at?!" With wireframes, users intuitively understand what you are trying to show them.
3. Wireframes help *you* to focus on what matters: the words. To illustrate this, take one of your pages, select all the text, and paste it into a plain text editor. You may be surprised at what you see. (For many websites, this exercise is much more useful than it may sound.) Some pages are

so beautifully designed, it's easy to overlook the words. But the words are what win A/B tests.

Ten years ago, the best way to create wireframes was with paper and Post-its. Some people still prefer to work that way. However, there is now an abundance of good software for doing it.

The following wireframing tools make it easy to display your work-in-progress designs. Some of them allow you to create working prototypes. Many of them allow you to create pixel-perfect final designs. Some even output production-ready code:

The tools that we use most often are Sketch, Balsamiq Mockups and UXPin. However, there are a crazy number of good alternatives, including...taking a very deep breath...Adobe Brackets, Antetype, AppCooker (for iOS apps), Appery.io (outputs code for mobile and responsive apps), Atomic.io, Axure (a complex, sophisticated wireframe tool suite), Balsamiq Mockups, Canva, CanvasFlip, Craft, Creately, Demonstrate, draw.io, FileSquare, Fireworks, FlairBuilder (for apps, mobile-friendly), Flinto and Flinto Lite (mobile-friendly), Fluid (specializes in mobile), Framer JS (allows you to prototype and code apps for desktop and mobile),...gasping for air...Fuse, Gliffy, Handcraft, HotGloo, Indigo Studio by Infragistics, iPlotz, iRise, Justinmind (mobile-friendly), Keynote, Koncept App, Lucidchart, Macaw (outputs HTML and CSS), Mockflow (outputs HTML and CSS), Mockplus, MockingBird, moqups, Naview,

NinjaMock, Notism (works with video too), OmniGraffle, Origami Studio, Patternry (for designing style guides),... starting to go blue in the face, gasp...Photoshop Wireframing Kit (templates for commonly used wireframing elements), Pidoco, POP (lets you upload your pen-on-paper prototypes and make them clickable), Principle, Power Mockup (a mockup and wireframe toolkit for PowerPoint), Proto.io, ProtoPie, ProtoShare, ProtoSketch, Prototyp, Prott, Real-time Board, Sketch (very popular, a successor to Fireworks),... feeling lightheaded, gasp...templates for paper sketches, UXPin, Visio, Webflow, Wireframe.cc, WireframeSketcher, and Wirify (a wireframing tool that lets you turn any existing website into a wireframe in one click).

The following are tools for people who like to draw by hand: Apple Pencil for iPad Pro, iskn, livescribe pens, Paper and Pencil by 53, and Penultimate.

6. Use design-feedback tools (to make it easier to test your designs)

Design-feedback tools like Verify (mobile-friendly) and five-second test allow you to get quick feedback on what you've created. Alternatives include IntuitionHQ and PickFu.

Here's how they work. You upload your designs or ideas, and then ask the panel for feedback in a variety of formats:

- **Five-second test:** The user is shown your design for five seconds. They then answer questions that you set them, like "What do you remember seeing?"

- **First-click analysis:** You set the users a task, and then see where they click first. The aggregated clicks are displayed as a heat map.
- **Question test:** You ask the users questions about your design.
- **Multiclick test:** You link several pages together and then set the users a task. The software records how the users navigate your website.
- **Annotation test:** You ask the users a question—for example, "What do you like and dislike about this design?"—and then ask them to annotate their feedback onto your design.
- **Preference test:** You upload two designs—two headlines, for example—and ask users which they prefer. Preference tests force the users to choose from two alternatives. They can provide insights that would take years with A/B testing. You just have to bear in mind that the insights are based on the users' opinions, which possibly may not correspond to their actions.

All of which can provide invaluable insights.

Regardless of how your designs were created, InVision app (mobile-friendly) allows you to easily turn them into functional prototype websites. You upload your page designs to InVision, and then link them together to make the site navigable. Then, you can carry out user tests on what, to the users, appears to be a real website, even though it hasn't seen a smidgen of code. Alternatives that have this functionality include Concept.ly and Marvel.

InVision app (mobile-friendly) also allows other people to give written feedback on your **work-in-progress designs**. You upload your designs, and then invite others to annotate them with whatever type of feedback you desire. Notable has similar functionality. **Alternatives** include Notable Prototypes (a variation of Notable), Firefly and BugHerd. Composite connects to Photoshop files, turning them into clickable prototypes.

To gather feedback on your **work-in-progress *videos***, you can use Frame.io, a fantastic web-based platform. **Alternatives** include Wipster, Symu, Vidhub, Remark, and Kollaborate. Such services provide great benefits; it's hard to gather and record such feedback even when everyone's in the same room.

Optimal Workshop provides several tools (OptimalSort, Treejack, and Chalkmark) to help you **optimize your website's navigation and information architecture**. The tools are described in our article about card sorting. **Alternatives** for card sorting include SimpleCardSort, UsabiliTEST, and Xsort.

Usability underpins all conversion

Almost every win has great usability woven into it—just like most successful books have "good grammar" in them. Usability underpins all conversion.

Along with readability, usability is a life skill that's worth developing. The world has no shortage of things that are infuriatingly confusing to use.

If you can make things easy to use, the world will love you.

Winning websites…give people what they want: here's what to do if your website doesn't satisfy your visitors' needs

For over ten years, we have been urging companies to dominate their markets. In fact, that's one of the main things that we help our clients to do. Many of them are now leaders in their verticals. In this chapter, we describe a powerful growth strategy that's hidden in plain sight. It's used by many of the web's most successful companies, it's ridiculously effective for dominating an industry, and yet many companies overlook it.

It's based around a major conversion killer: lack of interest.

Here's what we mean by "lack of interest":

- Visitors to your website can't find what they want.
- Maybe because you don't even offer it.
- So they leave.

What can you do about that? *Should* you do anything about that?

In this chapter, we hope to persuade you that it's *imperative* that you do something about it. And then we go on to describe a step-by-step process for implementing this strategy—a strategy by which many companies wipe out their competitors.

"Monopoly is the condition of every successful business." —
Peter Thiel, venture capitalist and cofounder of PayPal

How superstores—and leading e-commerce stores—use this principle to gain a formidable advantage

It's crucial that your company becomes the dominant player in its industry, by satisfying as many of your visitors' intentions as possible. If it doesn't, another business will take that space, capture those economies of scale, and push your company out.

Most superstores sell a huge number of products. If a visitor wants bananas then, yes, the superstore has bananas. If a visitor wants pet insurance then, yes, the superstore sells that too. And if a visitor wants children's T-shirts then, yes, it sells those too. By satisfying all of the visitors' intentions and desires, the store mops up more of the money that the visitors are willing to spend.

The preceding approach has a huge impact. If you can satisfy twice as many of your visitors' intentions, you effectively halve the cost of acquiring a customer. (Because the cost of acquisition gets divided over twice as many purchases.) Plus, if a visitor can get everything they want from you, they are less likely to visit one of your competitors.

For contrast, let's consider an imaginary company that *couldn't* easily adopt the above strategy. Let's call it "One Trick Squirrel." One Trick Squirrel makes nothing but smooth peanut butter. It doesn't even make the type with bits in. (It disposes of the bits in a landfill site.) One Trick Squirrel Peanut Butter could be the best in the world, but a One Trick Squirrel store could never be large, because it satisfies only one need—and few people want all of their weekly groceries to be peanut butter.

There's a limit to how large a store can become if it doesn't satisfy many visitors' intentions. Amazon began to do this early, presumably because many of its senior team members were from the retail industry, so they understood this economic imperative. So if you visit Amazon.com and search for a book called *Soils of Outer Mongolia*, you will find what you need.

Amazon created Amazon Marketplace to ensure that whatever a visitor wants, Amazon can provide (even if it's via a marketplace seller). Amazon understands the importance of giving visitors whatever they want. It's good for financial reasons, but it's also great for the visitor experience. And it means that Amazon is often the first place that Amazon's customers look—to the extent that some people forget that there are alternatives. Amazon is now nicknamed "The Everything Store"—and that was by strategy, not by chance.

How to do gap analysis for visitor intentions: a practical process that can generate breakthrough results

We use the following process to identify—and quantify—the opportunities for satisfying a website's visitor intentions.

Begin by using an on-page survey to ask your visitors why they visited your website:

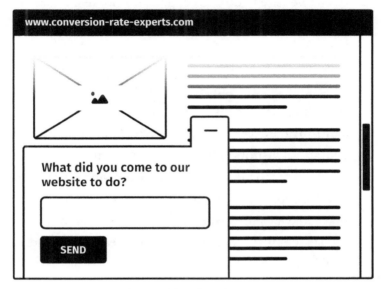

An on-page survey to identify your visitors' intentions.

Wait till you have collected at least a hundred responses. Then create a table with the following columns:

VISITOR INTENTION	PERCENTAGE OF ALL VISITS (%)	DO WE SATISFY THIS INTENTION?	HOW DO WE CURRENTLY MONETIZE THIS INTENTION? And how could we?	HOW MUCH REVENUE DO WE CURRENTLY GENERATE FROM THIS? And how much could we?

Table headings for gap analysis of visitor intentions.

- **Column 1: Your visitors' intentions.** In this column, list all the responses to the question "What did you come to our website to do?" Of course, no two responses are the same, so you'll need to group all the responses that had similar meanings. (For example, if one response was "Buy pet insurance" and another was "To see if I should get pet insurance," you might want to categorize them both as "Pet insurance.")
- **Column 2: Percentage of all visits (%).** Enter the percentage of visitors who gave each response.
- **Column 3: Do we satisfy this intention?** Enter a yes or a no, depending on whether this is a visitor intention that your website satisfies. For the example above, if you did sell pet insurance, you'd write "Yes." If you didn't, you'd write "No."

You may find that you satisfy only a small percentage of your visitors' needs.

Most companies don't think beyond this point. If the visitor wants pet insurance, and the website doesn't offer pet insurance, the company dismisses the visitor as having been unqualified.

However, the opportunity comes when you add the following two columns:

- **Column 4: How do we currently monetize this intention? How *could* we monetize this intention?**
- **Column 5: How much revenue do we currently gener-**

ate from this? How much revenue *could* we generate from this?

Columns 4 and 5 allow you to estimate the opportunity cost, revealing how you could increase your profit per visitor. For new products, you will have to estimate the value for Column 5. You can base your estimates on knowledge of your competitors' sales; information from suppliers; sales figures from a trial run; or calculations based on the survey responses, making assumptions about conversion rates.

Why is it so important to increase the profit per visitor? Because for many websites, the key metric is the acceptable cost per acquisition, which is how much you can afford to spend on acquiring each visitor. And that figure depends on how much profit you can generate from each visitor. So...

- if you can increase your profit-per-visitor,
- you can afford to spend more per visitor,
- and thus outbid your competitors on ads,
- which means you get the lion's share of the traffic.

Of course, conversely, if your competitors can monetize your visitors better than you can, then there's a good chance they can do the same to you.

(It might sound mercenary to talk about "monetizing visitors." However, from a visitor's-eye view, monetization tends to be a good thing; as a consumer, you'll find that there's a large correlation between the companies you like and the ones you give money to.)

How to populate Column 4—an easy way to generate ideas for monetizing visitor intentions

The following methods may help you identify products and services that would satisfy your visitors' intentions:

- **Method 1:** Temporarily add a Google AdSense box to the page. AdSense is powered by auction bidding, so the ads that are shown will be those that the advertisers (and Google) are confident will persuade your visitors to spend money. Once the ads are live on your website, study which products and services they promote.
- **Method 2:** Look at which products and services your competitors offer—particularly those that they push hard.
- **Method 3:** Identify companies that have similar economics to yours, and look at which products they cross-sell. Perhaps your company sells a B2B commodity, like safety signage. If so, look for other companies that sell B2B commodities, and see what other products and services they offer. You may be inspired to discover that the domain registrar GoDaddy cross-sells office productivity software. Or that the printing company Vistaprint cross-sells an email-marketing service. Not only will this reveal products you should be cross-selling, but you may also discover that the similar companies (like

GoDaddy)—or even the cross-sold companies (like the office software)—should be cross-selling your products.

An easy, risk-free way to add products and services

If your research reveals that you should be selling pet insurance, you don't need to set up an insurance company overnight. The following process allows you to explore tentatively how you could offer a new product range. The steps are listed in terms of increasing risk and commitment:

- **Continue running ads on your page:** If the ads are generating significant revenues, you could continue to run them. Some of our clients make a significant fraction of their revenue from displaying ads.
- **Continue advertising other companies' products, but bypass the ad network:** Contact companies that are advertising on your page, and do deals with them directly. They can pay you on a cost-per-impression basis, or on a performance basis with a cost-per-acquisition deal or a cost-per-lead deal.
- **If you believe that it would be strategically wise**, you may choose to handle more of the value chain in-house—by stopping the ads and instead designing, manufacturing, or providing a similar product or service yourself.

An example of creating additional product ranges

While studying Morphsuits' analytics, we noticed that many visitors were searching for a type of Halloween suit that didn't exist. Armed with the data, Morphsuits started manufacturing the new type of suit, safe in the knowledge that there was zero risk in creating it. The new suit became a top seller. We weren't surprised. We even knew approximately how many it would sell.

The Morphsuits team is extremely dynamic and has taken this principle far. Over the past few years, they have rebranded into MorphCostumes and increased their number of suits from 71 to over 300.

Winning websites...make the benefits clear: if your visitors aren't persuaded of the benefits, here's what to do

Even if your visitors can understand your writing...even if they can use your website...and even if you offer what they came for...they may not understand—or like—your value proposition.

In this chapter, we describe how to increase your conversion rate by fixing three of the most common problems with value propositions.

What is a value proposition?

Your value proposition can be defined as the benefits of your product or service minus its costs.

Value Proposition = Benefits – Costs

The costs aren't limited to the financials; they also include economic risk and the cost of time and resources.

A more buyer-centric definition of value proposition

The previous definition can be a bit too seller-centric. To aid clear thinking, we also find it useful to think of a value proposition as perceived through the eyes of an individual buyer. This view reflects more accurately what happens when a purchase is made:

- The decision is made in the mind of the buyer.
- The value of each feature will be different for each buyer. For example, some car buyers will find value in an ash-tray; others won't. Either way, it's clear that the "value" being discussed is the value to each buyer. Thus, in the customer's-eye definition, the value proposition is different for each buyer.
- Buyers' reasoning tends to be in terms of pros and cons, not benefits and costs—just listen to your own reasoning next time you buy something. If you create mental "pros and cons" lists and not "benefits and costs" lists, then it seems a shame to switch to the benefits-and-costs view when you're being a marketer, thus abandoning your lifetime of intuition.

Value Proposition = Pros − Cons
We find it useful to view a value proposition both ways—

through the seller's eyes and the buyer's eyes—as two sides of the same coin.

Let's start by focusing on the pros:

Three ways companies fail to communicate their benefits (the pros)—and several ways to fix the problems.

1. It's a myth that you should always talk in terms of benefits and not features

Some marketing experts say that all sales copy should be expressed not in terms of *features* (a product's properties) but in terms of *benefits* (how the product helps the user). This isn't true. You should sometimes state the features, sometimes state the benefits, and often state both.

The "always talk in terms of benefits" myth came from an observation that when buyers read features, they often think, "So what?" They don't understand how the features will help their lives. People looking to buy ebook readers, for example, might discover that a particular ebook reader has the feature of cellular connectivity. But the buyers may not understand how cellular connectivity would be useful. They would appreciate an explanation of how cellular connectivity would allow them to buy and instantly download books from anywhere in the world—on vacation, for example.

Sometimes, even obvious benefits are worth stating. Buyers might understand that a flight will take them to a beach, but an explicit mention of that benefit will still psychologically take them there. It activates those neurons.

However, there are times when you shouldn't explicitly mention benefits. One of them is when the benefit is taboo. A charity website shouldn't explicitly say, "Donate today and you can show off to your friends and probably go to heaven." Another is when the benefit is so obvious—or unimpressive—as to be a waste of words, and possibly patronizing. On a car manufacturer's website, it's probably worth mentioning that a car has a maximum speed of 120 mph, but it wouldn't be worth explaining the benefits of that.

The second half of "mention benefits and not features" is clearly nonsense. You should usually state features. Imagine a laptop manufacturer's website that says, "Lets you store loads of files" but then refuses to state the size of the hard drive. Benefits alone can leave the reader thinking, "Yeah, right." Benefits usually need proof to support them, and features are the most compelling type of proof. It's not enough to hear that a car is "really, really safe." You want to know it has air bags.

So when *shouldn't* you mention features? You should omit them when the benefit is not in doubt—or when there is little space and the benefit is better supported by a different type of proof. With fitness videos, for example, customers are much more persuaded by celebrity endorsements and by testimonials from other successful customers than they are by what's in the video itself.

As with most aspects of CRO, you become more effective when you ignore rules like "Technique X is good; Technique Y is bad" and instead understand the technique's function. Now that you understand the function of features and benefits, you'll be able to spot when to state a feature, when to state a benefit, and when to state both.

2. Many companies don't make it clear what their products or services do

Some products or services—particularly those that are complex—can be hard to describe. When such products are sold using a traditional brand-marketing approach, the results are often disastrous. The visitors don't buy because they don't understand what they'll get.

For example,

- **Unclear branding waffle:** "Music, Meet Home."
- **Copy that wins:** "The world's leading speaker system: Play any song in any room from any phone."

and

- **Unclear branding waffle:** "Introducing the oases of freshness: The Aquaris, the Tritona, the Anapos."
- **Copy that wins:** "Choose your water filter jug: a slim one for the fridge, a large one for the table, or a watertight one for on the go."

and

- **Unclear branding waffle:** "Express yourself. Impress yourself."

- **Copy that wins:** "The ultimate suite of cloud-based tools for all your marketing communications."

You get the idea.

If you are asked to improve the website of a technical product that is currently being sold with a brand-marketing approach, here's a useful tip: see if the product has a Wikipedia page. The Wikipedia page is likely to contain valuable plain-language descriptions that are absent from the manufacturer's landing page. Plain language almost always beats branding waffle.

Many marketers aren't aware that their website has this problem. The problem goes beneath the radar because visitors seldom report that they are "struggling to understand the value proposition." Instead, they say things like "I'm still researching." Also, most unclear descriptions aren't as obviously bad as the ones above. The best way to identify unclear benefits is through user testing. During user tests, listen for clues that the users haven't understood the product or service. For example, you may find that a user's objections to buying don't make sense. Or that the user has gone quiet.

Unclear product descriptions are guaranteed to kill conversions. So whenever we spot them, we know that a big win is just around the corner. Clarifying the benefits of complex, hard-to-explain products has led to many of our biggest wins.

3. Some companies forget to mention some valuable benefits

The travel-phone company Mobal gave away a high-quality travel adapter with every phone. But it forgot to mention the travel adapter anywhere on its website. When we added the travel adapter to the website, sales increased. So we added it to the offline marketing campaigns too. This was one of the many contributing factors that allowed us to triple Mobal's sales in one year.

We used this technique to great effect when we created more than $1 million of additional sales for Moz. In a case study on our website, we describe how we added to Moz's landing page many features that previously went unmentioned.

To ensure that you aren't making this mistake, list all of the elements of value that your visitors get, and then check that your website communicates them all clearly. It can help for you to order the product yourself, so you see the whole package with your own eyes. Also, ask your customers why they bought, and then ensure that all of their reasons are featured in your marketing materials with appropriate prominence.

4. Many companies don't make it clear what happens once the visitor says yes

Many websites—particularly those that sell services—don't help their visitors to envisage the postorder experience. There are many ways of overcoming this problem. The following method, common in Japan, is **rarely seen in the Western world.** Japanese consumers expect to be shown what they are going to get. All Japanese restaurants, for example, have plastic food in their windows, showing what each meal looks like.

Similarly, many Japanese companies display cartoon flowcharts that show what will happen once a visitor orders the product or service. We created the following flowchart for Mobal, to show Mobal's Japanese customers what to expect once they had ordered a travel phone.

A future-pacing flowchart for a travel-phone service.

The flowchart makes it clear how the process works: the order is placed, the phone is delivered, the phone is charged, the person flies abroad, calls are made, Mobal sends an itemized bill, the person returns home, and then the whole process is repeated for subsequent trips. The cartoon was so effective on the Japanese website, we transferred it to Mobal's USA website, to similar success.

Such flowcharts are an example of what the hypnotism world calls *future pacing*: The buyer is told what they are going to experience over the next few days, weeks, or months. (This is closely related to the sales technique of making the prospect "think beyond the sale.") Even though future-pacing diagrams are less common in the West, they are extremely effective here, because

- **They answer the questions that the visitors are asking:** "If I order this product or service, what will happen next? What will be the process I follow?"
- **They allow the visitors to rehearse mentally** the process of using the service, visualizing it as being part of their lives.

So if your product or service has an unclear postsale experience, then a future-pacing flowchart may help to increase your sales. We frequently get wins by adding them.

Future-pacing videos and how to create them

Once you have created a future-pacing diagram, you may find that it would benefit from being turned into a video. If so, remember that the process of creating a video should be no different from the process of creating a webpage. To begin, create the video in a low-res, highly editable format, which you can test on users—just as you would do with a webpage wireframe. If your video designer isn't comfortable carrying out user tests (in our experience, most aren't), you may prefer to do it yourself, as follows:

- Create your storyboard using the animation functionality of PowerPoint or Google Slides.
- If you wish to add a voice-over, record it in ScreenFlow.
- Iteratively test the draft video on users until you are confident that it communicates the message clearly.
- Only then should you get a high-quality version made.

This process will ensure that your final video will convert visitors.

The previous techniques provide four opportunities for optimizing your benefits and pros. In the next chapter, we will describe how to optimize the other side of your value propositions: the costs and cons.

Winning websites...have irresistible offers: if people aren't persuaded it's a great deal, here's how to optimize what they'll get

Even if your visitors can easily understand your value proposition, they may be turned off by the way the value is packaged and presented. The success of Facebook relative to Classmates.com—as parodied in The Onion—reveals how disastrous it can be to get your pricing model wrong.

This chapter contains a list of tips, strategies, and things to consider to grow your profits by optimizing your pricing and offers.

As you read the following points, we recommend you make notes of how each of them might apply to your business.

Establish your long-term strategy for pricing

- **Deciding what and how you will monetize.** (Classmates.com, for example, chose to charge a monthly fee, whereas Facebook chose instead to monetize from ad revenue.)
- Does your market benefit from economies of scale? (Most do.) If so, your ideal pricing strategy may be **penetration pricing**—charging a low price, basing your financial model on eventually reaching market-dominating economies of scale on the supply side and demand side:
  - **Supply-side economies of scale:** The more you sell, the higher your profitability.
    - As you sell more, your **cost of sales** (unit costs) usually becomes lower.
    - As you sell more, your **overheads** become relatively smaller.
  - **Demand-side economies of scale:** The more customers you get, the more value each customer gets from your service, for the following reasons.
    - You may benefit from having a **network** of customers. For example, if a phone system had only

two users, only one type of call could be made. If it had twelve users, sixty-six different types of calls could be made. The overall value of a phone system to its users is roughly proportional to the square of the number of people with phones.

- You may benefit from there being a market of **complementary products and services.** The project-management web app Basecamp has many integrations, which it promotes on its website. At the bottom of the page, it shows off how quickly it's acquiring new users, to persuade other companies to add integrations.

- You may benefit from having a **bigger knowledge base, more forums, or more trained users.** The ecosystem of knowledge around a product can be valuable in itself. WordPress grows partly because it's easy to find a WordPress developer and it's easy for those developers to find answers to their questions.

- **Perception that yours is the standard:** Users are aware of the value of choosing the ultimate winner—especially when they have to commit time and resources to your company—so they will be attracted by the perception that you'll win.

· **Price high at first, then lower prices:** This approach is good at mopping up all the money available in the marketplace. A book can be launched in hardback only, thus commanding a high price from those who are willing to pay it, and then later it can be released in paperback to mop up mass-market sales. This approach tends to be more effective with products (e.g., consumer electronics) than as a strategy with platforms (e.g., online stores). It also allows statements like "Used to be $XXX" to be used in the future advertising.

· **Communicate that prices will keep increasing:** This approach provides a kind of scarcity. It encourages buyers to act now, because they know prices will increase. It is useful when the major challenge is getting visitors to act promptly.

How to price the product

The following three principles are useful when considering how to price a product.

1. Consider the gaps in the market

Which market segment isn't currently being served? High-end customers? Low-end customers? Enterprise customers? Small businesses? Occasional users?

To your target market, what represents value? (Gillette succeeded by being first to acknowledge that no one wants to pay for the razor handle—they want to pay per shave.)

What would their "dream product" be? We find it's useful to ask yourself, "What would definitely work if only we were prepared to do it?" Write it down, even if it's miles from being possible. Once you know what it is, you may be able to think creatively about how you could offer it. This approach led us to create the highly successful $49 world phone, with no monthly fees, which became the standard in the world phone market.

2. Price high or price low?

For a given product or service, pricing low and pricing high each has its advantages. The challenge is to work out where on the continuum your winning strategy lies:

- **Low prices** lead to high conversion rates, more repeat purchases (or higher customer retention), high tell-a-friend rates and word-of-mouth, and favorable reviews.
- **High prices** lead to high profit per visitor, and thus a greater amount you can afford to spend to acquire customers—so you can spend more on advertising, pay more to affiliates and salespeople, etc.

Neither of above two options is intrinsically better than the other. Bear in mind that, in any market, there can only be one cheapest option—and that many people don't *want* the cheapest option: most people don't buy the cheapest car available, the cheapest shampoo available, the cheapest clothes available, the cheapest watches available, and the cheapest insurance available. They tend to buy options they perceive to be of higher value. There are many opportunities for the high-profit-margin option, provided you can find features and benefits that customers would be willing to pay a premium for. A good mindset is to imagine that you will charge a premium price, and then use your marketing knowhow to justify that price.

Note that many companies take external investment to fund their costs of client acquisition in the short term. The investment gives them all the previously mentioned benefits of high prices and low prices, and is based on the assumption that the strategic benefits of growing quickly will be worth it in the end.

Offer strategies

Once you have decided on your pricing strategy, you are ready to start packaging up your offers. Here are some of the many options available to you:

Lead with a "no-brainer"

Decide at what point in your offer sequence you monetize your services. The winning strategy is usually to defer gratification, making the initial purchase a "no-brainer," and then make money on the subsequent payments:

- **Make the headline offer irresistibly appealing.** This often involves understanding what main criteria your prospects are using to determine value. **Set low prices for the criteria people consider when judging value.**
  - **Charge low prices for the easily comparable aspects:** Supermarkets are very competitive on prices of comparable products, like Heinz baked

beans, and charge more for products that are less easy to compare, like artisanal balsamic vinegar.

- **Make your money on the things people don't consider when making a decision:** Restaurants often have low-priced meals, then make all their money on drinks.
- **Consider stripping down the features of your service**, then charging for extras. Car dealers often have a low headline rate, then charge for extras.

- It can help to make the **initial purchase free.** If you can't make it free, make it seem cheaper:
  - Offer a **"free trial,"** which may be a no-strings, **completely free sample**, perhaps with a discount voucher if they decide to continue. This works if your service is fantastic, and the best way to persuade buyers is to get them using it.
  - Offer a **free trial with an ongoing monthly charge** if the customer continues.
  - If it's not possible to offer a sample, consider **a simulation of a sample.** Freebird is a service that allows travelers to get an alternative flight if theirs is canceled. As part of Freebird's conversion funnel, it allows users to experience the whole process as a simulation, to demonstrate how easy it is.
  - Consider offering **something small and irresistible for an amazing price**, just to get something into the buyer's shopping cart. Once the buyer has accepted

that they'll be going through the checkout, they are more likely to buy other things.

- ○ Offer an **initial discount** (e.g., only $9.99/month for the first three months; $19.99/month afterward).
- ○ **Multibuy deals:** Buy one, get one free is effective— more effective than "half-price," because it keeps a high price on the product (so doesn't lower its perceived value) and encourages the customer to buy twice as much. The same goes for other types of multibuy deals.
- ○ State that "**We won't bill you until** N days after your purchase."
- ○ Allow the buyer to pay in **installments** (e.g., three monthly payments of $9.99). This works well if your research reveals that many buyers don't currently have the money to pay for the product outright.
- Allow the buyer to "**return it within X days for your money back.**"

Other principles for creating the offer package

- An **ongoing monthly fee** almost always beats taking a one-off charge. It represents less initial risk for buyers, and customers pay as they receive value, which feels more reasonable.
- Ensure that the first product that people buy is one of **your most liked ones.** This will make customers much

more likely to return. Survey customers to ensure that you know which of your products are most liked. (Note that your most frequently bought product isn't necessarily the ones that's most liked.)

- **Upsell and cross-sell.** Creatively think of other things that the buyer would pay for, such as:
  - better service;
  - better customer support;
  - insurance;
  - extra information (e.g., a valuable ebook);
  - quicker or better service;
  - complementary products they'd also buy (for inspiration, study the conversion funnels of companies that sell commodities in highly competitive markets like domain names, business cards, and cell phone plans;
  - for inspiration, ask customers (maybe via a survey) what other services they'd like you to offer and what other related services they currently use.

Add premiums (free gifts) and incentives

- **Information** is a good thing to give away as a premium, because it has zero (or almost zero) costs of sale and can have incredibly high perceived value. Think of valuable information that your customers would love to have. For example, someone buying a health supplement to help them sleep may highly desire a report that describes how to get a good night's sleep. You can deliver the information in a wide range of formats, including audio, video, electronic or printed reports, software, tools, or access to websites.

- If some of your offering involves information, consider how the information can be made to **educate the buyers** about how to buy your type of product, and how to appreciate the ways in which your product is superior. This works well in B2B sales, because B2B buying is often complex. For example, a seller of web hosting can benefit from giving away a guide called "7 Mistakes to Avoid When Choosing a Web Hosting Solution."

- Consider offering particular premiums only **to customers who spend more than a certain amount**. One of our favorite techniques is to offer a valuable free report for customers who buy one unit, an additional free report for customers who buy three units, and a further free report for customers who buy five units. A buyer who wants that third report can never get it if they always order one unit at a time. This offer alone can greatly increase the average order value.

- If a customer is paying with **someone else's money** (such as their employer's), consider options that will reward the person personally. Companies that sell to businesses often use the following rewards such as meals, events, air miles, cash back, and gift vouchers. (Of course, don't offer anything that's unethical or illegal.)

- Offer premiums to **encourage prospects to behave in**

a certain way. For example, if you want all the orders to be placed via the web, or via the phone, offer a premium for people who do so.

- Offer discounted prices if people order quickly (e.g., early bird discounts) or in large quantities.

Versioning: Different prices for different people

It helps to have different pricing for different people:

- **Many customers have a price in mind** before they begin, and will pay that price regardless. (A friend of ours went looking for a suit, expecting to pay about $700. He found one that looked good, but it cost just $70. He decided against it, preferring to stick to his plan of finding one that cost more. Imagine how frustrated the store owner would have been to know that not only did she not sell the suit, but that she *would* have sold it if she had charged ten times as much for it.)
- **Create pricing segments for each of your groups of customers.** For example, you may choose to have different prices for enterprises, small businesses, and domestic consumers. Then, start from the point of view of the customer: begin with the price they'd be prepared to pay, and then work out what the product or service should be at that level. Ensure that each price level contains a "deal maker" or "deal breaker"

component that makes it worth it for the buyer to pay the extra amount.

- **Consider a price that's ten times your current highest price**, and then decide what people would pay. A company that advises people on getting work permits may charge $500 per client. The company might benefit from exploring what a $5,000 service would entail. Who would use it? Even if only a small fraction of buyers took advantage of such an offer, the effect on the economics of the business could be significant.

- **Bestow status levels upon your customers:** Have different levels of customers, and publicly reward those on the higher levels by giving them a higher status. People are naturally competitive and aspire to become better customers. This technique is used by every producer of luxury goods. Even credit card issuers manage to charge more for premium gold and platinum cards.

- **Offer a loyalty program**, whereby the buyers get certain rewards once they have purchased a certain number of units from you. This encourages them to return for more, thus forming a habit, and increasing your lifetime customer value. As every cafe knows, it helps to give customers free loyalty points to begin with, so their reward account has value from the outset.

A/B testing your prices

Testing pricing can be a thorny issue. Some users may contest it. However, changing pricing is one of the most surefire ways of increasing (or decreasing) a company's profits, so there's a high value in doing it (and a high cost to getting it wrong—which is a good reason to A/B test it).

One effective option is to run A/B testing to offer different prices to different users, but then, once they have ordered, to charge them all the lower price, to make it fair. Bear in mind that—as with all A/B testing—buyers who use more than one device may see different versions of your pricing.

Another (less scientific) option is to test different prices on different days or weeks.

In both cases, it can be hard to measure the results if your buying cycle is long.

How to communicate the offer

Sometimes, you don't need to change the offer or the value proposition; it can be enough to change how you describe it. The following techniques work well:

- **Position yourself as—and actually be—the prospects' trusted advisor,** so they know you're acting in their best interests. This is *incredibly* important—be very careful not to squander your integrity for the sake of one quick sale.
- Make prices look larger by displaying the decimal points ("Free gift—**a $29.00 value**") or lower by hiding them ("**Costs only $29**").

- Odd prices work slightly better: **$9.99 is perceived as being disproportionately lower than $10.00.** This is presumably for the same reason that people get excited when their car odometer clicks over to 10,000 (even though it's just another mile), and sad when they reach their fortieth birthday (even though they're only a day older than they were the day before).
- If a price has been reduced, put a slash through it to avoid confusion, so it's clear that it's not the current price. So rather than saying "Was $119, now only $89," say, **"Was $119, now only $89."**
- **If something is free, and the offer sounds too good to be true, mention that's it's free several times, in different ways.** For example: "It's free, so you pay nothing, no strings attached, no hidden charges, absolutely no cost to you whatsoever."
- **Many people don't understand percentages**—at least not at a gut level—so it's much better to say "half-price" or "one-third off" than "50% off" or "33% off."
- **Use apples-to-oranges comparisons** to remind people what great value the product is. If you're selling a training course, compare it to the cost of a college education, and show people who have gone on to get jobs, to highlight the net benefit. If you're selling a shed, compare it to the cost of having a house extension. If you're selling a video conferencing solution, compare it with the price of international travel. You can make almost any product sound like a great deal by comparing it to the price

of something the buyers are already squandering their money on, like lattes or beer. Which makes you wonder how anyone manages to sell lattes or beer.

- **Consider expressing the price in a way that makes the numeral less:** like changing a monthly rate to a daily rate.

Give a reason why you're making such a great offer

Buyers don't always want the cheapest option (e.g., a Casio digital watch), but they do want a bargain (e.g., a Rolex Submariner for only $3,000). However, a bargain needs a good rationale. If the deal is great—as it should be—explain why, with proof. The following approaches can help:

- "Our prices are great because **we cut out the intermediaries** and sell directly to the consumer."
- "This is an **opening sale.**"
- "This price is a **special product-launch price.**"
- "This is a special offer for **new customers.**"
- "This is a special offer for **existing customers.**"
- "This is an **end-of-line clearance promotion**" (the offer is about to change, and there's scarcity).
- "This promotion is **linked to a certain event**" (e.g. Christmas, summer, back to school or Black Friday).

In all cases, give indisputable proof. If the product was previously sold at a higher price, give details (when, where, how much)—and justify why that price was reasonable. If it's cheaper or better than competitors' products, give details, maybe with a comparison chart.

Payment options

Different customers tend to have different preferred methods of ordering and paying. It's often best to offer the ones they are most comfortable with:

- **Payment method**
  - Credit card or debit card
  - PayPal, Google Checkout, Amazon Pay or Apple Pay
  - Direct debit or standing order
  - Purchase order
  - Credit card over the phone
  - 0% finance
  - Check
- **Payment schedule**
  - Pay in **multiple installments** (which is good when the initial price point is high).
  - **Till the person cancels**: if your service is charged on a monthly basis, you keep charging the customer until they cancel it. You may choose to specify **a minimum term**, before which the customer may not cancel. (This is popular with telecoms providers.) The length of the minimum term (e.g., twelve months, eighteen months, or twenty-four months) can affect the take-up rate.

- **If your service has a monthly charge**, consider also offering an annual charge at a discount of, say, 15%. This will do several things:
  - It'll be great for your cash flow.
  - Customers will not cancel early (there are loads of reasons why a customer may cancel early—their situation may change, they may prefer to switch to your competitor, their needs may change).

Change the offer

Regularly changing what you offer can have one big advantage: Visitors have a reason to come back, just to "see what's new."

However, make sure you're changing the offers for customer-centric reasons (track the performance) and not just because you're personally bored and want a change.

Winning websites...are trustworthy: if visitors are wary, here's how to make your website a powerhouse of credibility and proof

What if your visitors don't trust you?

Sometimes, visitors don't proceed because **they aren't persuaded that your company is any good.**

This is usually because your website lacks relevant trust signals. There simply isn't enough proof that the visitors should use you. This chapter describes some highly effective ways to use proof to improve your company's credibility (and sales).

What kind of proof should you add? There are tens—maybe hundreds—of ways to show trust and credibility. Some of them are particularly suited to certain types of businesses, but most businesses benefit from the following:

Size and growth rate

Visitors are greatly influenced by the size and success of companies. For daFlores, Latin America's largest network of florists, we gained a 44% uplift in sales by highlighting how many Facebook fans the company had.

We demonstrated the huge size of daFlores by highlighting its army of Facebook fans.

Reviews and testimonials (particularly from authorities and experts)

In one experiment for a software company, we grew sales by over 20% by creating a page that linked to hundreds of customer reviews. (We gathered the reviews by surveying the client's customers.) The visitors were persuaded by hearing the experiences of people like themselves.

The following image shows how one company took a bold approach by highlighting its worst reviews:

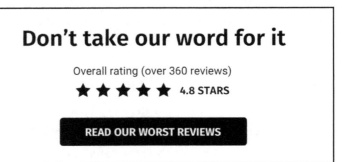

Don't take our word for it

Overall rating (over 360 reviews)

★ ★ ★ ★ ★ 4.8 STARS

READ OUR WORST REVIEWS

A bold approach: We know of one e-commerce company that demonstrates its integrity by highlighting its worst reviews.

Data and statistical evidence

Buyers are much more likely to believe your claims if you support them with hard data.

So if you sell cat food, it's not enough to say that cats like the taste of it. Why would people believe you? A popular cat food brand supported its claim with data: "Eight out of ten owners said their cat prefers it."

Insurance companies don't say, "We make it easy to save on car insurance." They support their claims with data, like: "15 minutes can save you 15 percent or more on car insurance."

Restaurants that deliver fast food don't say, "We'll be there as fast as our bikes can carry us—we promise." They say things like "Delivered in 30 minutes—or it's free."

Hand soap manufacturers don't say that their product "Kills a *lot* of germs." They say, "Kills 99.9% of germs." It sounds much more convincing.

And in its 1962 ad, a particular oil refining company didn't just say "We supply a lot of oil." It said, "Each day, we supply enough energy to melt 7 million tons of glacier!"

With hindsight, maybe that last one was misjudged.

Celebrity associations

Celebrity associations can be more effective than you might expect. When selling a diet, for example, many people will be more influenced by a celebrity figurehead than by scientific research.

Over the years, we have paired several of our clients with celebrity figureheads. Most of the celebrities allow their image to be used in return for a fixed fee for a specific duration. In one case, the celebrity was happy to do it for free, because she was a fan of the company.

A word of warning. Before you commit to a deal, though, you may choose to first run an A/B test to measure how the celebrity affects conversions. One of our clients had a celebrity figurehead whose presence actually *reduced* sales. The client's branding agency hadn't carried out A/B tests (we've yet to see one that does), and so was oblivious that they had caused such damage.

Demonstrations

Sometimes, the best way to prove something is to demonstrate it.

A poster showing the space required to transport seventy-two people by either car, bus, or bicycle. The photos demonstrate, better than words ever could, how single-occupancy cars take up a disproportionate amount of road space. (Image credit: Cycling Promotion.)

Social proof

In our case study about how we grew Crazy Egg's conversion rate by 363%, our winning landing page featured some of Crazy Egg's prestigious clients. Similarly, when we made over $1 million for Moz, one of our winning pages had a headline that incorporated the names of some of Moz's prestigious clients. Buyers are reassured when they see that others similar to themselves have already chosen—and like—a particular company.

It can help to mention your most prestigious customers. Readers think, "If it's good enough for those companies, it's good enough for me."

Two industries in which trust is particularly important

Trust is more important in some industries than others. Visitors to health and fitness companies and to financial institutions tend to be particularly concerned about trust—because choosing an unsuitable company could be calamitous.

- Health and fitness companies typically benefit from being associated with medical professionals, celebrities, research institutes, and universities.
- Financial institutions tend to benefit from displaying proof of their longevity and size, and from demonstrating flawlessness.

"Proof magnets": A way of bolstering trust and credibility

The world already contains a vast amount of proof of your company's merits, much of which you probably take for granted. Across the web, there will be a lot of content that *would* persuade your visitors if only they were to see it. Search for reviews of your company, testimonials, positive PR, etc., and you'll probably find that only a fraction of this proof ever gets seen by your visitors—either because it's not on your website, or because it's tucked away in the corner of a dusty "About Us" page.

Make sure your visitors see this proof, by incorporating the best of it into your most-visited pages.

We have helped one of our clients, TopCashback, to win the Fast Track 100 award three times in a row.

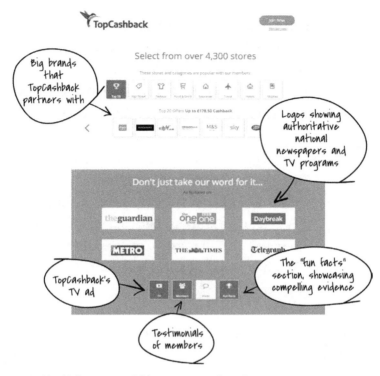

TopCashback's homepage exhibits many types of proof.

TopCashback's homepage features many types of proof:

- **Big brands** that TopCashback partners with, segmented by category (e.g., fashion, travel, and hotels).
- The tabs at the bottom of the image link to
  - logos showing authoritative **national newspapers and TV programs** that TopCashback has been featured in;
  - **testimonials of members** describing the benefits of using TopCashback;

- ◦ **TopCashback's TV ad**, which is both informative and persuasive (plus, the fact that it's a national TV ad is itself evidence of credibility);
- ◦ **the "fun facts" section**, which is actually a showcase of compelling evidence that TopCashback is the best at what it does:
    - "We pay the highest rates: You'll typically get at least 5% more cashback with us."
    - "If you find a better rate elsewhere we'll match it."
    - "We were the first cashback site in the world to pass 100% of the cash to our members."
    - "We have the most offers" (with statistical evidence).

Combined, these elements are enough to convince the most skeptical of visitors that TopCashback is trustworthy and authoritative.

Taking it a step further: Proof investment

Beyond proof magnets lies *proof investment*. Once you understand what would persuade your visitors, then you should spend time, money, and ingenuity acquiring those things. For example...

- If your visitors would be most persuaded by
    - ◦ **an association with a Hollywood celebrity**...then invest in acquiring that;
    - ◦ **rave reviews from experts**...then work to gain them;

- ◦ **your rapid growth or huge size**...then set that as a goal;
- ◦ **awards**...then aim to win awards.

This illustrates an important point: **conversion is not an afterthought. Conversion is identifying what type of company your visitors would ideally love to do business with...and then becoming that company.** This approach goes to the core of your business. It means that your customer research determines the direction in which your company grows.

As it should.

Hence, the company's product strategy and marketing strategy should be led by its conversion team.

What if visitors trust your company but not your product?

Just because visitors trust your website doesn't mean they have found a product that they trust. A visitor may be happy to use your online pharmacy, but they still need to be persuaded of the efficacy of a particular drug.

A visitor may lack trust for several reasons:

- · **The product isn't good.**
- · **The product isn't described well enough.**
- · **The product isn't the best choice for the visitor**—perhaps because the search functionality or navigation has done a bad job.

In such cases, your job is to persuade the visitor of the merits of the *product*, but not at the expense of eroding their trust in your *company*. Leading e-commerce companies are great at this. They retain their trusted-advisor status by including impartial customer reviews.

The same types of proof that were effective for building trust in your company are equally effective at building trust in a product. Just be aware that "lack of trust in your company" and "lack of trust in the product" are two separate problems. Both must be solved before a customer will place an order.

Winning websites...remove risk: how to use guarantees to remove visitors' fear of commitment

A guarantee can be powerful, like a chainsaw.

Used right, it can cut through customer objections.

Used wrong, it can cut through profits.

In this chapter, we'll describe how to know if a guarantee would work for your business—and how to design and implement a guarantee that works.

When (and why) do guarantees work?

Guarantees don't always increase sales. To understand when a guarantee would help, consider the two major functions of a guarantee:

Function 1: A guarantee **reduces the risk** for the customer. If the company doesn't fulfill the guarantee's promise, the customer is compensated.

Function 2: A good guarantee **self-evidently promises that your business will be harmed** if you don't honor your claims. It effectively says, "Our promise must be true. Otherwise we wouldn't be in business." It thus acts as a kind of **proof.**

Many people underestimate the importance of Function 2.

So guarantees are effective when...

- **the visitors want what the company is promising,**
- but they are **nervous about the risk,** or are **skeptical about the claims,**
- and **your service lives up to its claims.**

In such cases, the new guarantee can have amazing results. Just by adding and perfecting a guarantee, we boosted one of our client's sales by almost 50%.

A guarantee would not be effective for a hot dog cart, though. Because visitors aren't nervous about wasting a few dollars on a hot dog. And hot dog carts don't make claims that make visitors skeptical.

However, if a hot dog cart were to claim to sell "the best hot dog you've ever tasted," then a guarantee would help to overcome the prospects' natural skepticism. And if the cart were to increase the price of its hot dogs to $10, a guarantee (such as "$10 for the best hot dog you have ever tasted—or it's free") would help to reduce the customers' risk, and therefore increase the sales.

Ingredients of a highly effective guarantee

A great guarantee contains the following ingredients:

- It should guarantee that **the customer will get the benefits they desire.** (In fact, you may consider charging in terms of the benefit—like razor blade manufacturers make their money on the blades, not the handle.) And it should **address the main risks** about which the buyer is tentative. If the buyer is worried about whether the product will achieve a particular result, offer a *performance guarantee*. If the buyer is worried whether they'll be happy, offer a *satisfaction guarantee*. If the buyer is worried about whether the price is good enough, offer a *price-match guarantee*. A guarantee will be effective only if it addresses an existing concern.

- It should **offset the risk**—and ideally neutralize it—so, if things go wrong, the buyer will be compensated for their time, effort, and cost.

- It should **have a name**, indicating that it's a tangible thing. For example, "Our 100% Money-Back Guarantee" or "Lifetime Guarantee." The name makes a good headline.

- The best guarantees are worded positively. They don't say, "If you dislike our service..."; they say, "We guarantee that you'll love our service." **The most common mistake with guarantees is to word the guarantee negatively—as a "get-out clause"—rather than in positive terms, as a promise.** When you bring up the subject of returns, use a phrase like "In the unlikely event that…"

- **Explain why you can afford to make the guarantee**—because you aren't really taking a risk; most customers are delighted.
- Sometimes it helps to put the guarantee **in the voice of the company's chief spokesperson.**
- Consider giving the guarantee a **long claim period.** A guarantee with a deadline is effectively a time-limited offer. The buyer has a certain number of days to make a decision. If your guarantee's claim period is short—fourteen days, for example—the principle of urgency will be strongly working against you. On the other hand, increasing your claim period from twelve months to twenty-four months doubles your financial risk with possibly no incremental increase in conversion rate. The optimal period depends on many factors, including your costs of sales, the quality of the product, the time a customer perceives they will need to evaluate the product, the typical lifetime of the product, and the impracticality of returning the product. To identify the optimal duration, we find it useful to use financial scenario modeling supported by A/B testing data.
- At the point of sale, it should be evident that your guarantee is **easy to invoke.**
- Emphasize that **no strings are attached.** In particular, customers often worry that the guarantee will be nul-

lified if they use the product—or even take it out of the box—so emphasize that they are encouraged to use it.

- Promise you'll give a **prompt refund**. Customers worry that it may take a long time to get the money back.
- The guarantee should be **featured at all the points where the buyer is thinking of the risk**. That's usually near the call to action. Sometimes, it's up front, too. You may also choose to mention it when they abandon.

A nine-step checklist for implementing a guarantee safely

Is your company hesitant to offer a bold guarantee? That's understandable. A guarantee can do harm if it's implemented badly. Also, with guarantees the feedback loop is long, because you can't calculate the costs of invoked guarantees until after the guarantee period has expired.

The following workflow provides a low-risk way to implement a bold guarantee:

1. **Create the guarantee**, based on the principles described previously.
2. **Carry out scenario modeling, as follows:** Create a table in which the columns represent different values of "uplift in conversion," and the rows represent different values of "percentage of customers who invoke the guarantee." Then work out the net change in profit for each combination. Also consider how guarantee claims would

be handled operationally (accepting returns, restocking shelves, issuing refunds, etc.). If you are satisfied that the guarantee will generate additional profits, then proceed to the next step.

3. **Run the guarantee as an A/B test for a short time**—for just a few days, if that's all the risk you can bear.

4. **Wait for the guarantee period to expire.**

5. **Calculate the increase in profits,** based on the measured uplift in sales.

6. **Calculate the cost of people invoking the guarantee.** In our experience, the invocation rate tends to be lower than companies expect, sometimes by an order of magnitude.

7. **If you need more data (which you probably will), return to Step 3** and run the guarantee for longer. By doing this in small increments, you remove the risk caused by the long feedback loop.

8. **If you do have enough data,** and the increase in profit more than offsets the cost of returns, make the guarantee permanent.

9. **Return to Step 1,** creating a bolder guarantee.

The most fruitful activities regarding guarantees

We've had wins from many types of guarantees: price-match guarantees, satisfaction guarantees, payment-deferral guarantees—even weather guarantees. The wins typically come from three activities:

1. **creating a guarantee** for a company that doesn't already offer one;
2. **improving the wording** of a guarantee (some guarantees should be compact, and some should be long);
3. placing the guarantee **at the right point** in the conversion flow.

If risk is a factor for your visitors, then those three activities are likely to be effective for you.

The boldest guarantee we have tested

While we are on the subject of guarantees, you might be interested to hear about the boldest guarantee we ever tested. It was for the travel phone company Mobal. Previously, using financial modeling, we had correctly identified that Mobal could make huge profits by selling each phone at a subsidized price, and then making all of its money from subsequent call charges. So each time we sold a phone, we made a significant short-term loss. Offering a guarantee on such an offer might have sounded reckless.

Because the stakes were so high, we carried out a scenario analysis. It forecast that a guarantee would be likely to increase the overall profits, even taking into account the costs of servicing the guarantee. (This is where it helps to have a Cambridge PhD scientist on your team.)

Fortunately, our modeling paid off. We tested a sixty-day satisfaction guarantee—which was even longer than the average customer's trip. The conversion rate rose, and the return rate turned out to be much lower than our safeguards had allowed for—so the guarantee was a huge success. Before long, the conversion rate was so high, Mobal was able to invest profitably up to a quarter of a million dollars per month in offline advertising, and the sales tripled within twelve months to $9.1 million.

Winning websites...are like water chutes: if your website doesn't appeal to both early- and late-stage buyers, here's how to design unbeatable multistep funnels

It's easy to forget that some visitors aren't ready to buy

You hear marketers say that they "want to make visitors reach for their credit cards." But pushy selling is usually thrashed by a sophisticated, relationship-building funnel.

In this chapter, we explain why you need to develop a sophisticated multistep marketing funnel, which converts even those visitors who are "just browsing." Then, we present the CRE Funnel Planner, a framework that makes it easy to design sophisticated funnels.

What we can learn from bricks-and-mortar bookstores

About twenty-five years ago, offline bookstores learned not to push the hard sale. They discovered they could convert a visitor from "just browsing" to "buying" by making their stores highly conducive to reading. They added chairs, reading areas, and even in-store coffee stores. They discovered that the more time that visitors spent in the store, the more likely the visitors were to buy.

Amazon has adopted the same approach, allowing visitors to "look inside" books.

The Hazelnut Trail—a mental model that helps you to design amazing conversion funnels

Imagine that you lost your beloved pet squirrel after letting him off the leash during a walk in a nearby forest. How would you coax him back home to his room? One effective approach (according to the animal advisors we hired for this convoluted analogy) would be to leave a trail of hazelnuts from the forest all the way back to the house.

If you simply left all the hazelnuts in a large pile back at home, then your squirrel wouldn't make the journey. The plan would work only if you left a trail of evenly spaced, irresistibly high quality hazelnuts from where the squirrel was last seen to where you wanted him to be.

The Hazelnut Trail is a useful analogy for an effective marketing funnel. Like squirrels, people tend to act based on rewards, especially short-term rewards. In his book *The Hidden Tools of Comedy* (which we love), Steve Kaplan says,

> "Everything we do, we do with the hopeful (at times deluded) idea that it will improve our lives. Everything we're wearing today, every choice we've made, we made because we thought it would, even infinitesimally, make things better for us."

Your conversion funnel should be like a Hazelnut Trail. Your visitors must be irresistibly attracted by each step of your sales funnel. They must believe that every step will make their lives at least slightly better.

The Conversion Rate Experts (CRE) Funnel Planner makes it easy to plan your Hazelnut Trail

All of the previous advice is easier said than done. The CRE Funnel Planner provides a valuable framework. It helps to turn your one-step sales process into a much more sophisticated, more profitable multistep process. It also makes it easier to communicate your funnel to your colleagues.

The planner has the following three columns:

The CRE Funnel Planner: Much more powerful than you'd guess from those three simple columns.

A (terrible) one-step funnel for a seller of fishing boats

Now, let's populate the CRE Funnel Planner for InflataFish, an imaginary company that sells inflatable fishing boats. Badly.

WHAT THE VISITOR WANTS	WHAT THE COMPANY WANTS	HOW TO DO IT
• To look at inflatable fishing boats	• Get the visitor to click on the "Buy now" button (or order by phone), then pay.	🌰 Sales copy

A CRE Funnel Planner for an imaginary seller of inflatable fishing boats.

InflataFish has a **crude one-step sales process:**

- **The visitors want to look at inflatable fishing boats,** maybe to buy one but at the moment just to look.
- **InflataFish wants to get the visitors to click on the "Buy Now" button** or order by phone, then pay.
- **So InflataFish has overzealously reached for the visitors' credit cards.** It has created a sales page (represented by the hazelnut-shaped bullet point) that describes the boat and its features, advantages, and benefits. InflataFish hopes that the visitors will click "Buy Now" and spend $2,000 on a boat.

It's equivalent to going to a nightclub and asking a stranger to marry you.

A (good) multipart funnel for a seller of fishing boats

InflataFish would benefit from creating a **multistep Hazelnut Trail,** as follows:

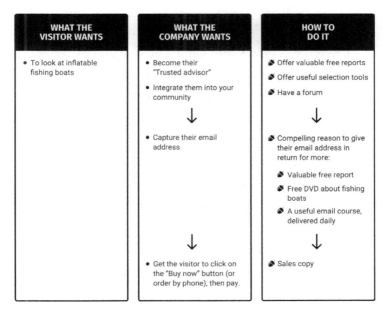

WHAT THE VISITOR WANTS	WHAT THE COMPANY WANTS	HOW TO DO IT
• To look at inflatable fishing boats	• Become their "Trusted advisor" • Integrate them into your community ↓ • Capture their email address	🐿 Offer valuable free reports 🐿 Offer useful selection tools 🐿 Have a forum ↓ 🐿 Compelling reason to give their email address in return for more: 🐿 Valuable free report 🐿 Free DVD about fishing boats 🐿 A useful email course, delivered daily
	↓ • Get the visitor to click on the "Buy now" button (or order by phone), then pay.	↓ 🐿 Sales copy

A much-improved Hazelnut Trail for the same company.

In this case, the left-hand column is still the same—the visitor just wants to look at inflatable fishing boats. And, as before, InflataFish ultimately wants the visitor to click the "Buy Now" button.

But now, InflataFish has set itself many intermediate goals, each of which offers an appealing hazelnut reward:

- First, InflataFish wants to **become the visitors' trusted advisor**. It could do this by providing valuable free reports that explain how to buy inflatable fishing boats. And it could provide useful product-selection tools. Both of those are high-quality hazelnut.
- Then, it wants to **integrate the visitors into its com-**

munity. It could do this by providing a forum in which its visitors could share fishing advice and experiences. That's another high-quality hazelnut.

- Then it wants to collect **the visitors' email addresses.** Which it does by providing three compelling offers (hazelnuts), including
  - a valuable free report called *"How to plan the ultimate fishing trip—100 great tips from our customers."*
  - a free, useful DVD about buying and using fishing boats.
  - a useful email course delivered daily called "Angling Alerts: The latest news for fishing enthusiasts."

Then InflataFish wants the visitors to **click on the "Buy Now" button** and pay for a boat. The visitors will do this when they are ready. But only because over a period of hours, days, weeks, months, or even years, they have gradually moved through the Hazelnut Trail, always to the point that matches their level of comfort, desire, and readiness.

It's naively optimistic to hope that all visitors will go along the whole trail in one step. Business relationships—like personal relationships—take time to build.

"Readiness"—an important concept to understand

The word *readiness* is important when it comes to conversion funnels. Many marketers forget that, to a large extent, buyers will buy only when they are ready.

- Sometimes people become ready *because of something that has happened*. For example,
  - A cell-phone contract expires, so a person becomes free to choose another carrier.
  - On deciding to move house, a person starts to look for a moving company.
  - After eating too much over the holidays, a person decides to join a weight-loss program.
- Sometimes people become ready to buy **only once they have started a project**. For example, people tend to plan a vacation on a day of their choosing, not when they see an ad for travel insurance. As soon as they decide to start planning, they begin a flurry of buying flights, hotels, car hire, etc.

How to manage readiness

It can be prohibitively expensive to persuade visitors to buy when they aren't ready. It's economically preferable to accept that buyers will buy when they are ready.

There are two ways in which a travel company can get a person's attention when they are ready:

1. **Appear in the prospect's mind at the right time.** By building a relationship with a prospect, a company can be the first thought that pops into a prospect's mind when they become ready.
2. **Appear somewhere in the buying process.** For exam-

ple, a company that sells travel insurance could ensure that its marketing materials appear within the marketing funnels of other travel companies (such as hotels, airlines, travel insurance, airport transport, etc.).

A sophisticated, $125m Hazelnut Trail

To see an excellent example of a Hazelnut Trail, visit MoneySavingExpert.com, which is a UK-based financial services company. Its website is extremely popular, getting 13 million unique visitors a month. In fact, one in six UK citizens has opted in to its email list. In 2012, it sold for £87 million (about $125 million).

It's not even obvious that the website is a commercial venture. On arriving at the website, you'll be invited to subscribe to the free money-saving email. Then, you'll be shown the valuable best-buy guides that explain, in plain language, how to buy different types of financial service. Then, you'll be introduced to the money-saving forum and many other useful tools.

The website's Hazelnut Trail is so effective you don't even feel like you're dealing with a company. By the time that you sign up for a financial product, you probably won't even feel like you have been sold to. The fact that the company gets paid at the end seems almost incidental.

Winning websites...manage complexity:
can your visitors not see the wood for the trees? Here's an eight-step approach to managing complex sales

When we ask a website's visitors why they didn't buy, we hear them say the same things over and over again. Lack of trust comes up a lot, as does lack of understanding and inability to find a suitable product.

However, some objections aren't widespread—they are product-specific. For example, there might be a hundred reasons why a buyer isn't ready to buy customer-relationship-management (CRM) software, and each of the reasons is specific to CRM software. Each objection has to be tackled individually. What can you do if your visitors have tens—or even hundreds—of different objections?

This is where conversion gets hard. For a marketer who was hoping just to add a few testimonials and a guarantee, the problem can seem overwhelming. It can only be solved by a combination of process, diligence, and skill. And the following steps:

- Step 1: A simple template to manage visitors' objections (and your counterobjections)
- Step 2: Should you use long or short copy? (Try to reduce how many words you need, by reducing the commitment. And then use as many words as you need.)
- Step 3: How to organize your persuasive copy using "separation of concerns"

- Step 4: Make it clear where one module ends and the next begins
- Step 5: Optimize your navigation
- Step 6: Two ways to improve how you label modules
- Step 7: How to use "progressive disclosure" to stop your visitors getting lost in the detail (and then abandoning)
- Step 8: Fallback options to convert users who still can't find what they need

If your business has many different objections, this chapter describes how you can overcome every single one of them. Some of the steps may seem obvious, and some may require a lot of discipline to implement, but together they represent the easiest way to grow many businesses.

Step 1: A simple template to manage visitors' objections (and your counterobjections)

In Section 2, we described how to identify your visitors' objections. To manage all the responses, we recommend you create what we call an "O/CO" table—a table with two columns, one for objections and the other for counterobjections. Here'sa template O/CO table:

OBJECTIONS	COUNTEROBJECTIONS

You can get an amazing amount of value from populating a simple table of your objections and counterobjections (O/CO).

To begin with, the visitor type and visitor intention should be broad—for example, "All visitors to ABC.com." However, if you work for a large enterprise—a national cell phone carrier, say—it may be something narrower, like "Visitors who are under contract with another carrier, who are looking for a new phone on a pay-monthly rate plan."

Into the objections column, add all of your visitors' objections, as revealed by your research. To make your list more manageable, you may wish to rank the objections by how frequently they get mentioned.

In the counterobjections column, write down the most effective responses you'd give to overcome each objection. **You can identify good counterobjections using the following techniques:**

- **Ask salespeople** how they respond to each objection.
- Look through the company's **sales training materials** and **sales scripts** to see whether there are prewritten responses to each objection. (If there aren't, the table

you are creating should be added to the company's sales training course.)

- Ask **live chat support representatives** how they counter each objection.
- See whether the company has **"canned responses" for live chat**. They can be a goldmine of tested counterobjections.
- **Come up with counterobjections yourself.** With most companies, this is the most fruitful method. The people who are best at coming up with counterobjections tend to be intelligent and diligent and have an obsessive knowledge of direct-response marketing techniques, persuasive copywriting, psychology, and usability—all the core skills of CRO.

Step 2: Should you use long or short copy? (Try to reduce how many words you need, by reducing the commitment. And then use as many words as you need.)

Your website will need to contain *at least* as many words as you'd use when selling face-to-face.

But this raises an important point. Selling what? If your company makes customer-relationship-management (CRM) software, you have a wide choice over what you sell at each stage:

- **At one extreme, you could aim to complete every-**

thing in one step, selling a three-year enterprise-wide contract for the CRM, with a multimillion-dollar commitment. This may require months of face-to-face meetings.

- **At the other extreme, you could sell an instant free trial with no credit card required**—and postpone the rest of the selling to a later stage in your conversion funnel. It may take you no more than a minute of conversation to sell a free trial face-to-face.

If you ask for less, you don't need to use as many words. So it pays to explore how you can redesign your conversion funnel so that each step becomes less commitment.

Of all the possible low-commitment steps, lead-generation (or lead-gen) pages deserve a special mention, because they are particularly effective. A lead-gen page is a page designed to collect the visitors' contact details—often their email addresses. The "submit your email address" field on a lead-gen page represents a low perceived commitment to the visitor, but a high value to you as a marketer—because it allows you to lead-nurture the visitor with long copy ad infinitum (or, at least, ad tedium).

Of course, if you lower the commitment at an early stage, bear in mind that you may have simply deferred the commitment—and the persuasion required—to a subsequent stage. Sometimes a free trial of the product or service does that persuasion well. Also, it allows you to collect the visitor's contact details. Sometimes a free trial doesn't work, though, especially if the product or software unavoidably requires the user to commit time or resources. (Commitments can include money, work, time, and risk.) Beware of suboptimizing a particular page only to discover that the problem pops up further down the funnel. A supermarket could get more customers to the checkout by getting the security guards to drag them there—or by closing off the rest of the store—but it wouldn't increase profits.

The most successful online retailers do both: They reduce the commitment required from the buyers by pricing products aggressively low, and then using many words.

In many situations, it's most effective to offer a dual path: to provide direct, low-commitment calls to action, plus long copy. Successful software companies often provide a low-commitment way forward (a free trial), plus detailed information for those who would prefer it. The calls to action may be scattered throughout the copy, as in the following image:

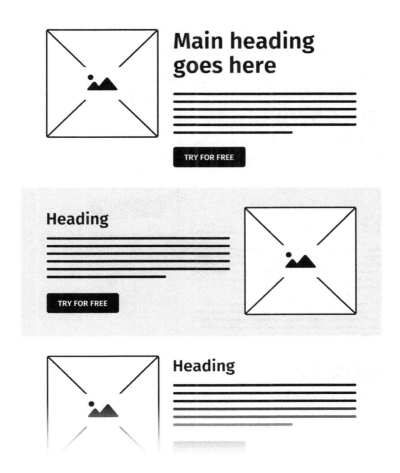

Main heading goes here

TRY FOR FREE

Heading

TRY FOR FREE

Heading

Many visitors want to know the features of software before they try it out, so it pays to provide two paths. You can push a low-commitment free trial but also provide pages and pages of information.

Alternatively, the call to action may be in a lead-gen form that's either static or scrolls down the side of the page:

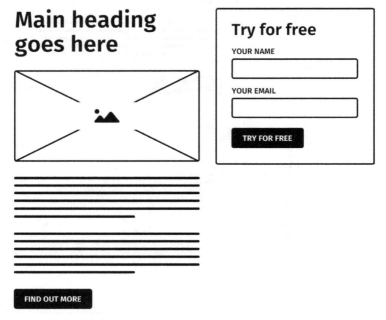

Your call to action may sit at the side of your long page.

You can offer as many paths as there are next steps that you'd like the buyer to consider:

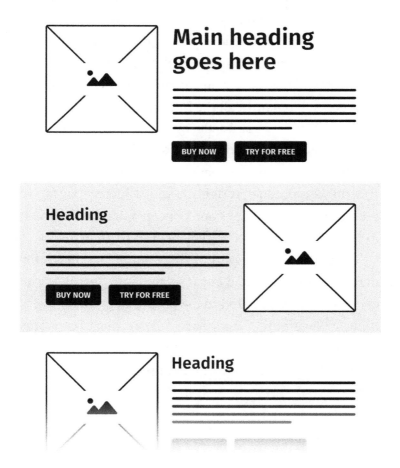

Sometimes it's optimal to provide multiple paths. This example has three: (1) An order button for visitors who are ready to buy, (2) a button for visitors who want to schedule a trial, and (3) pages and pages of information for visitors who want more details.

Step 3: How to organize your persuasive copy using "separation of concerns"

No matter how long your page is, your visitors should be able to easily find the information they need. They shouldn't have to read the whole page from start to end. **A webpage should be long like a phone book, not like a Russian novel.**

Your challenge is thus one of information architecture: How can you organize all the information so that visitors see what they need—and at the right level of detail—without getting bored? This is conversion at its hardest. It's one of the biggest challenges for many websites. It's also extremely fruitful when you get it right. In the following pages, we present some techniques and concepts that don't appear in copywriting books. They will help you a great deal.

Separation of concerns is a fancy name for when information is organized and encapsulated into modules. The concept is closely related to the phrase "a place for everything and everything in its place." Separation of concerns is essential when you're managing a lot of content. For website design, the modules can be paragraphs...

Main heading goes here with lead message

1ST FEATURE OR BENEFIT

4TH FEATURE OR BENEFIT

2ND FEATURE OR BENEFIT

5TH FEATURE OR BENEFIT

3RD FEATURE OR BENEFIT

You can encapsulate benefits into clearly labeled **paragraphs.**

...or page sections...

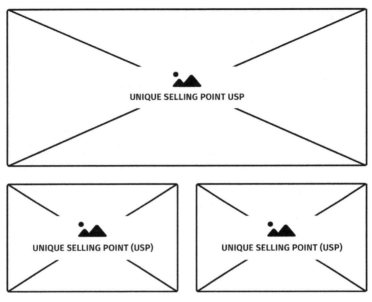

Many winning websites clearly encapsulate their content into separate **page sections**.

...or pages, or groups of pages...

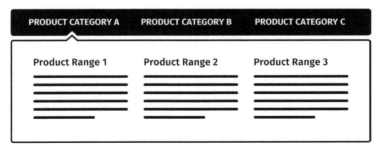

The navigation bars of many websites clearly encapsulate the content into **groups of pages**. (In one of our case studies, we describe how we used this technique to increase paid memberships for Smart Insights by 75%.)

By modularizing, you allow your visitors to easily find the information that they need, and to ignore the rest.

It's hard to stress how important it is to organize information into an architecture that's easy to navigate. **Once a visitor is lost, it's difficult to show them counterobjections. They'll never find them.**

Separation of concerns may seem obvious and straightforward, but once a company does it badly, a mess quickly ensues. We are fans of a particular brand of sit-stand desks.

However, whenever we recommend them to people, we struggle to find the version we own (there are over twenty variations, each with subtle differences). The problem is common to many e-commerce websites that give each product variation its own page. The visitor has to play a game of spot the difference between different product pages, many of which are almost identical except for a few differences.

Visitors don't want to play spot the difference. If they are buying a laptop, they don't want to browse product names like "ABC123-1Tw, ABC123-2Tb, etc." Instead, they prefer to see headings that reflect their current mindset and that narrow down the choices. They want to be given choices like "Do you want it with a 1 TB or 2 TB hard drive?" and "Do you want it in black or white?"

That's not a store—it's a warehouse! This is an example of how an e-commerce page should *not* look. A product page should help buyers choose between the available options. It shouldn't be just a database dump.

The following hack is useful if you are unsure of the logic by which your products or services should be sold: Phone the company's sales department, and ask an open-ended question like "I'm having trouble choosing which sit-stand desk to buy. Could you help me?" Then notice which questions the sales advisor asks. If they are good, they'll ask questions that narrow down the choices. If they are great, they'll have a mental logic tree that elegantly narrows down the choices in as few steps as possible. They almost certainly won't ask what the website asks: "Do you want Product ABC, Product DEF, or Product GHI?" Only a web marketer would do that.

There's one more reason to clearly modularize your content: **If information is hard to find for a visitor, it will also be hard to find for the website's editors. So it**

will be even more likely to deteriorate over time. Poor separation of concerns tends to snowball. Some telecoms companies' websites are messy to the point of being almost irrecoverably out of control.

Step 4: Make it clear where one module ends and the next begins

Once your information is clearly modularized, you need to make it clear where one module ends and the next starts.

You can do this using a hierarchy of text sizes and formatting, as we do in this book, using the following techniques:

- **Headings** (and subheads) clearly show the start of sections (and subsections). However, be aware that readers tend to be less aware of the structure than the writer is. Readers are typically fine with Heading 1 and Heading 2 styles, and tend to be just about okay with Heading 3 styles. By the time a page has reached Heading 4 or below, the readers often struggle to understand where they are in the hierarchy.
- **Paragraph returns** indicate minor changes of topic.
- **The opening sentence of a paragraph** often introduces the theme of the paragraph.
- **Text in bold (like this) reveals key points,** to help skim-readers.
- **Bullet-point lists (like this one) represent parallel ideas.**

Another way to group information is to **add background colors to page sections**.

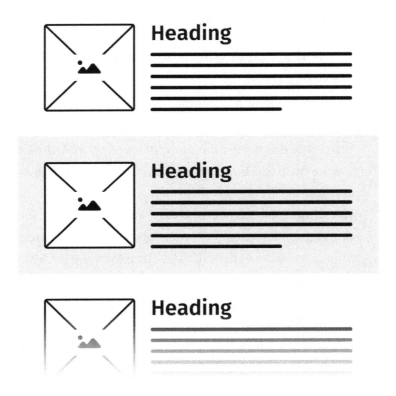

To make it clear where one section ends and another starts, try using alternating gray and white backgrounds. Imagine how much more confusing the page would be without the backgrounds.

Another way to demarcate sections is to **put information into boxes**.

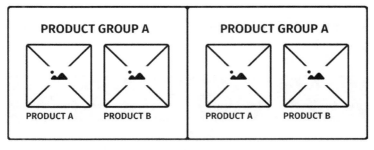

It helps to clearly encapsulate content into separate page sections—and it doesn't take up any additional space or require any additional thinking.

Step 5: Optimize your navigation

Good navigation helps users find the information they are seeking. Navigation elements include horizontal and vertical navigation bars, tabs within pages, and on-page Johnson boxes (like the list of links near the top of our article at www. conversion-rate-experts.com/design/).

Your navigation should reflect how your visitors would expect to find things. For example, for an e-commerce fashion retailer:

- Users first expect to segment by age/gender (e.g., "Women")
- And then by type of product (e.g., "Clothing")
- And then by subcategory (e.g., "Dresses")

The modularization should reflect the visitor's mental model—not the mental model of the website's creator.

When we doubled the sales of the web app PhotoShelter, we managed to grow the sales by 12% by optimizing the navigation:

PhotoShelter's visitors converted much better after seeing examples. So we added an "Examples" tab to the navigation bar, growing overall sales by 12%. (Image credit: PhotoShelter.)

If you are unsure how to organize your information, card-sorting allows your users to do it for you.

Step 6: Two ways to improve how you label modules

1. Label each module with a headline that's clear and descriptive

It's important to use the right words in a section's heading. Your words should concisely describe the contents of a section in a way that will be obvious to visitors. Unfortunately, many websites fail in this respect. In many websites' navigation bars, for example, the headings can be understood only by someone who's already familiar with the website. For example, companies often use the names of their products in the navigation, even when the names aren't self-explanatory.

You might find it useful to think of it as "surprise navigation." With surprise navigation, you don't know what you're going to get until you've got it. Surprise navigation is as pointless as a road sign that can't be understood until you've arrived at the destination. It's generous even to call it navigation; it's more like an in-joke.

Surprise navigation isn't limited to navigation bars; it also appears anywhere that has road sign functionality—including headlines, subheads, the titles of page sections and other page elements.

Surprise navigation is a common problem; it leads visitors into oblivion, and it kills conversions.

You can eliminate yours by reading all of your headings, including the tabs in your navigation, the headings of pages, and the headings of sections—and then ensuring that each heading would be understandable to a newcomer. Then, to confirm that you were right, carry out user tests and Treejack tests.

2. How to fix your headings: Many marketers mistakenly label modules with "categorizers" when they should have used "spoilers" or "teasers"

It's often not enough for a heading to describe what's in the module. It should also tease or spoil.

So if your page has a section of media testimonials, introduce it with a spoiler headline. That way, you communicate the message even to skim-readers:

- **Categorization headline:** "Media mentions" (worse)
- **Teaser headline:** "See what the press are saying about us..." (a bit better)
- **Spoiler headline:** "We've had rave reviews from TIME, CNN, and many others!" (much better)

If you definitely want the user to click through, use a headline that teases, not spoils:

- **Categorization headline:** "A video of a kitten pouncing on a hawk" (worse)
- **Spoiler headline:** "A kitten pounced on a hawk in a playful way, because they are friends" (no better)
- **Teaser headline:** "A kitten pounced on a hawk. I was expecting a nasty ending. What happened next is amazing!" (better)

Even many professional copywriters make the mistake of

using categorization headlines when they should have used spoiler or teaser headlines:

- **Categorization headline:** "Meet the 4th-gen ThinkoStat Learning Thermostat" (worse)
- **Teaser headline:** "The 4th-Generation ThinkoStat Learning Thermostat. See how we've made the best even better." (better)
- **Spoiler headline:** "Meet the 4th-Generation ThinkoStat Learning Thermostat: Now it controls your hot water, it's even more beautiful, and it's easier to use." (better)

Step 7: How to use "progressive disclosure" to stop your visitors getting lost in the detail (and then abandoning)

Progressive disclosure **means hiding information so visitors don't see it until they need it.** We rely heavily on progressive disclosure. It is still greatly underused.

On the web, **the most common method of progressive disclosure is to put information onto another page.** That way, the visitor won't see the information unless they click on a link to it. This method has drawbacks, though. Once a visitor clicks on a link to go to another page, they may not return.

It's often much better to use on-page elements.

Examples of progressive disclosure

There are many ways to hide information within a page so it's revealed only when the user hovers over it or clicks on it:

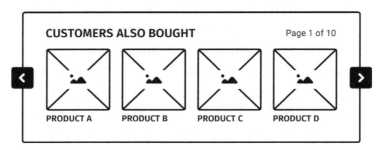

Carousels with right and left arrows indicate that more products can be viewed.

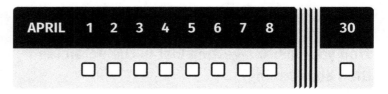

An accordion can be used to hide detail.

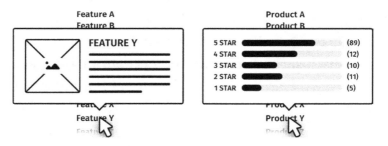

Tooltips are a great way to conceal information until it's needed.

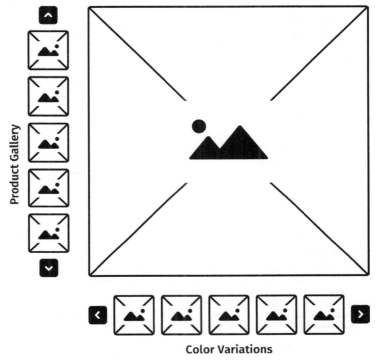

Color Variations

It's possible to use horizontal and vertical carousels in combination, to show two different dimensions of data. For example, in an e-commerce store, you could show thumbnails of color variations on the horizontal axis and photos of different views of the product on the vertical axis.

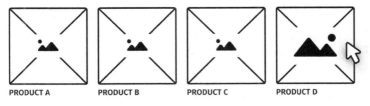

PRODUCT A   PRODUCT B   PRODUCT C   PRODUCT D

When the users hover over an image, an alternative view can be shown.

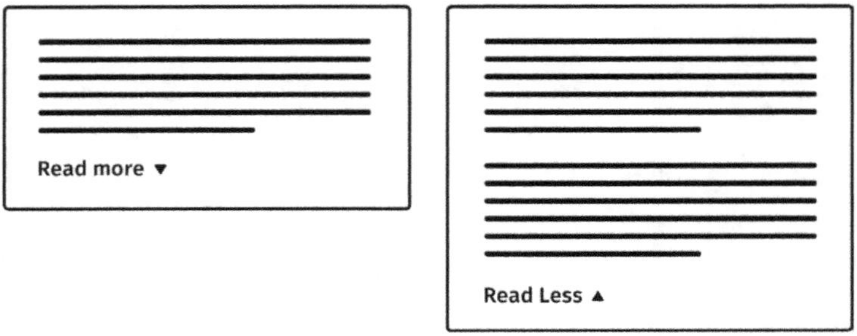

Read more ▼

Read Less ▲

Information can be hidden behind a "Read more" link (which, in the context of a bookseller, might sound like a subtly placed marketing slogan). When clicked, the "Read more" turns into "Read less" (which would be a terrible slogan for a bookseller).

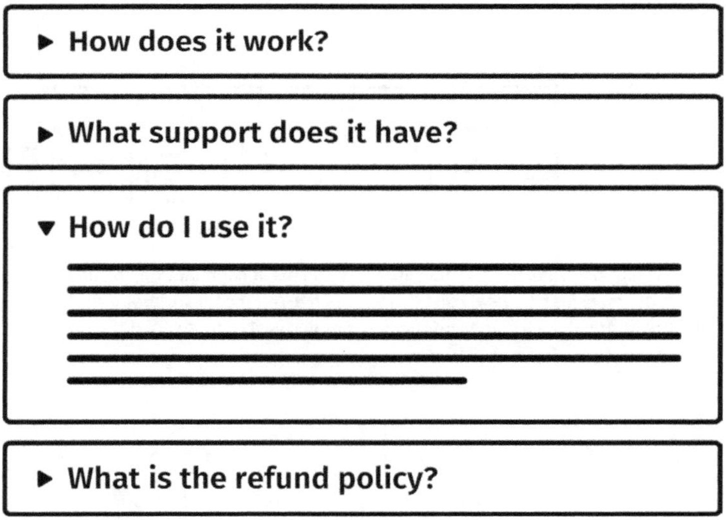

▶ **How does it work?**

▶ **What support does it have?**

▼ **How do I use it?**

▶ **What is the refund policy?**

The information in a Help Center can be intuitively categorized into subjects. When the user clicks on a triangle, the answer is revealed. You can keep the answers short by linking to separate pages for users who want even more detail.

DEPARTURE: JFK TO SFO

Fri: 6:10pm - Fri 7:30pm
Virgin America 592
Coach on Airbus A320

Layover (Palm Springs) 23h 15m

Sat 6:45pm - Sat 11:58pm
Sun Country 618
Cound on Sun Country 73G

Layover (Minneapolis) 16h 32m

Sun 4:30pm - Sun 8:10pm
Sun Country 247
Coach on Sun Country 73G

47HR FLIGHT TIME

A tooltip can contain any kind of information.

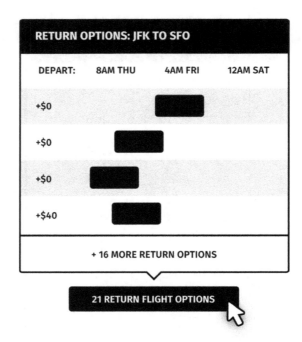

RETURN OPTIONS: JFK TO SFO

DEPART:	8AM THU	4AM FRI	12AM SAT
+$0			
+$0			
+$0			
+$40			

+ 16 MORE RETURN OPTIONS

21 RETURN FLIGHT OPTIONS

There's no limit to what can be put in a tooltip. A travel website may choose to display the times of return trips when the user hovers over the outbound journey.

Visitors to sunshine.co.uk were concerned that the company had no phone number. We wrote a counterobjection that explained why this perceived shortcoming was actually a benefit. We added "Where's our phone number?" to the header, and linked it to an overlay. This was one of the contributing factors that helped us make an additional $20 million (£14 million) per year for the company.

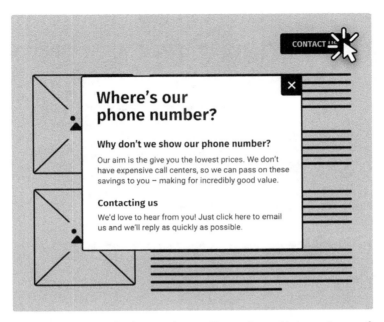

By keeping the information in an overlay, sunshine.co.uk was able to counter one of its biggest objections without distracting visitors away from its conversion funnel.

SimpliSafe is an innovative home security company. We have helped it to grow its revenue by more than five times. (Its team members are some of the smartest, most dynamic people we've worked with.) Because SimpliSafe sells self-install systems, its visitors need a lot of advice. In the following example, SimpliSafe hides a huge amount of information behind those turquoise plus (+) signs.

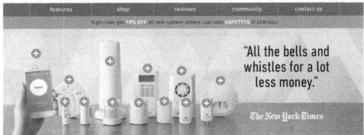

When clicked, each one of the turquoise "+" signs reveals a different overlay (as shown in the image below). (Image credit: SimpliSafe.)

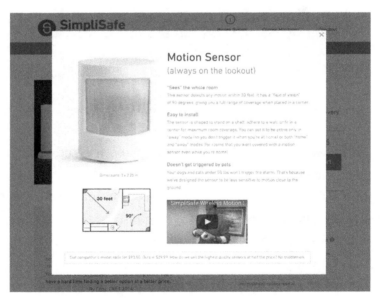

Each overlay contains enough information to warrant having its own page. But it's better for it to be in an overlay, so the user doesn't lose where they are in the conversion funnel. (Image credit: SimpliSafe.)

At the start of this chapter, we described progressive disclosure as hiding information. **However, it may be more** intuitive to think of progressive disclosure in the positive sense—as *adding* information that otherwise may not warrant space on the page.

There are so many ways to progressively disclose information, how do you know where to start? Should you use a tooltip or an exit overlay? In the following pages, we describe the four types of "building blocks" with which you can build progressive-disclosure elements.

Building blocks of progressive disclosure: 1. Ways to indicate that more information can be revealed

You can use any of the following visual text cues to indicate that more information can be revealed:

- **Arrows, triangles,** and **chevrons** indicate that information will appear as an expanding element. (The following image shows multiple types—not that you'd normally include all of them on one page.)

➔ How does it work?

▶ What support does it have?

▼ How do I use it?

❯ What is the refund policy?

- **Text that's made to look like a link**—usually by being a different color or underlined—is often effective and uses no additional space.

Lorem ipsum dolor sit amet, consectetur adipiscing elit. Nulla eu nisi arcu. Integer finibus sed orci a cursus. Sed ut tincidunt urna. Fusce sollicitudin nulla non elit convallis laoreet. Donec gravida elementum orci non dignissim.

- **Icons** with +, *?,* or *i* on them use little space and hint at the nature of the content that will appear.

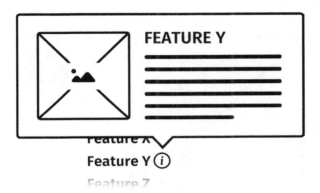

- **Magnifying glasses**, depending on context, can indicate that the resulting information will be zoomed in, or that a search field will appear.

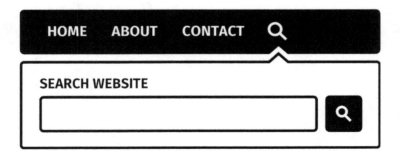

- **Nothing**—in other words, you give no clue that information will be progressively disclosed. For example, if a user hovers over a particular page element, a tooltip may appear unannounced. Take this approach if you aren't anxious for the visitor to discover the information, and you don't want to clutter the interface.
- **Showing elements that are abruptly cut off.** If only part of an element—a photo, for example—is visible, visitors correctly guess that the rest of it can be revealed. (This is one of the techniques we described on our website in our article about how to make users scroll down your page.)

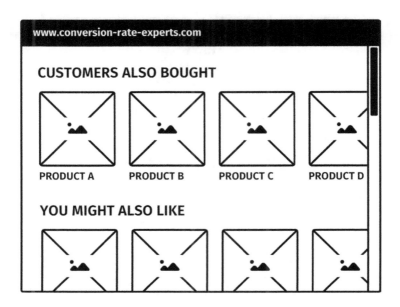

Building blocks of progressive disclosure: 2. Ways to trigger the information

The information can be triggered in several ways:

- By users **clicking** on the area. Use this if you don't want to show the information unless users are keen to see it.

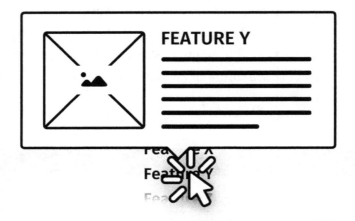

- By users **swiping**, as with carousels. (Consider offering **clickable arrows** too, to supplement the swiping.) Swiping is great for showing a large amount of extra information without disorienting the visitor.

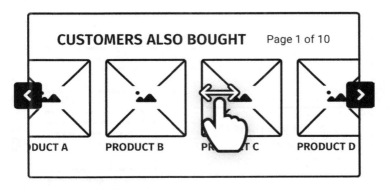

- By users **hovering** over the area. Use this option if you are keen for the information to be viewed. Touchscreens don't support hovering, so touchscreen users usually have to click instead.

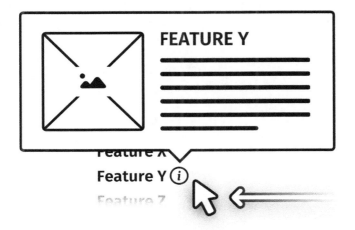

- When the user **scrolls** a certain distance down a page.

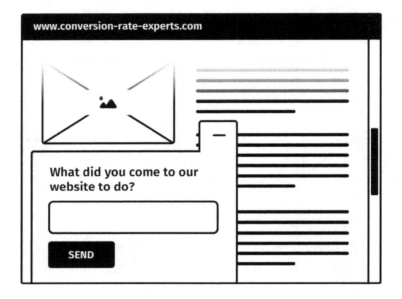

- When the user appears to be **exiting the page**, by moving their pointer above the viewport of the browser.

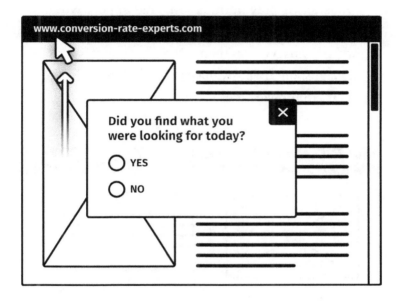

- Some websites effectively do progressive disclosure in reverse; they reveal the information spontaneously when the **page loads,** and then allow it to be hidden. Some websites display notifications that appear when the page loads and then disappear after a few seconds—or when the user closes them. Qualaroo's on-page surveys appear spontaneously but can be hidden by clicking on their "minimize" tabs.

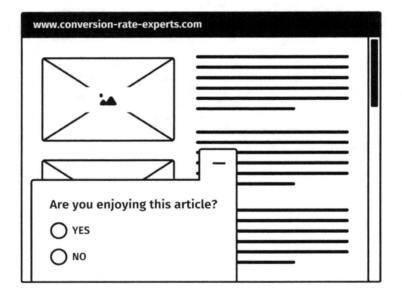

Building blocks of progressive disclosure: 3. Formats in which to present the information

The hidden information can appear in several formats:

- In a **separate page.** Do this if you aren't anxious for the visitor to return to the original page.
- In an **overlay.** Overlays can be effectively used if you don't want to distract the visitor from your conversion funnel.

- In a **carousel**. These come in useful when there's a lot of similar information to show.

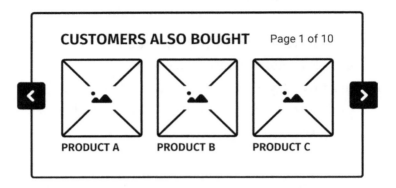

- In a **tooltip** (which is effectively a small overlay). These are great for small amounts of information. They tend to be anchored to a point on the page, so they can be fiddly when triggered near the edge of the viewport.

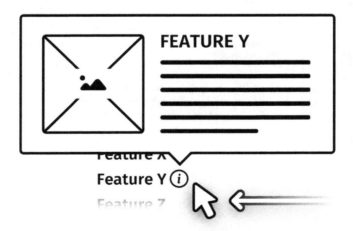

- By **a page section expanding** within the page. These are particularly useful when the information doesn't need to be hidden again. And when expanding them won't mess up the layout of the page.

Read more ▼

Building blocks of progressive disclosure: 4. Ways to trigger the information to be hidden again

The revealed information can be hidden again in several ways:

- By disappearing **when the user stops hovering** over that section. This can help or hinder users, depending on whether they are more likely to have problems continuing to hover over the content (because it's small) or hiding it (often because it's large). Hovering doesn't apply to touchscreens, for which clicking must be used instead.

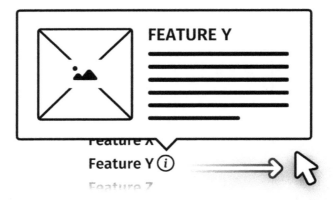

- By users **clicking on a "Close" icon.** This is often the best option; users tend to understand it well.

- By users **clicking away from the page element.** This is convenient for users who are "in the know," but it isn't discoverable, so it should be used in addition to showing a "Close" icon.

- Spontaneously **after a certain time period**. This is often used with information that appeared spontaneously too.

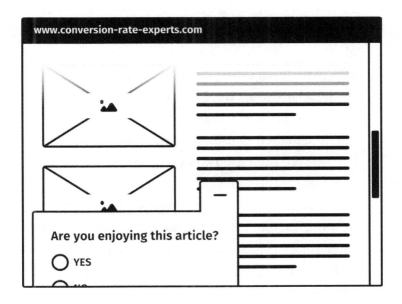

- When the **user stops doing** whatever triggered the information.

Step 8: Fallback options to convert users who still can't find what they need

Sometimes, visitors will fail to find information no matter how well you have structured it.

In such cases, **the following fallback options can be effective:**

- **A search box:** Search can help users to find what they need, but only at the expense of "teleporting" them into a different part of your website. Once they arrive on the search results page, they often lose their bearings. Once in a while, look through the queries in your search logs to identify which information the visitors had failed to find while browsing. Often, you'll find that the information wasn't where users would have expected it to be.
- **A knowledge base:** Knowledge bases can help users find answers to their questions. But, as with search boxes, visitors who search knowledge bases often lose where they were in the conversion funnel.
- **Live chat:** A live chat operator should be able to find information that the visitor can't. Whether live chat is economically viable depends on the economics of your business (and not on the whims of the customer-support team).
- **A prominently placed phone number:** Not all visitors want to pick up the phone. But for those who do, phone calls tend to convert extremely well. The main drawback of phone calls is that they don't scale easily; call centers operatives need hiring, training, paying(!), and looking after. As such, the ideal combination is usually for the website to do as much of the work as possible.

Winning websites...sail past the competition: if your visitors are choosing your competitors, here's how to win

If you don't have a strategy for winning *despite* competitors, you are doomed.

This chapter describes many powerful concepts and techniques we have used to help our clients dominate in some of the world's most competitive markets.

Some of the things you'll get in this chapter:

- four reasons **why niching usually wins**;
- **how to spot good niches**: three easy techniques you can use;
- six ways to spot **opportunities your competitors will ignore**; and
- some **funny photos** of good and bad competitive strategies.

How to make your visitors choose you (and not your competitors)

No company exists in a vacuum. Sometimes, visitors abandon your website simply because they prefer your competitor's.

How can you win the sale?

You could attempt to become better than all of your competitors in every way, but it's hard being all things to all people. It's much more effective to *niche*—to focus your efforts on being the best in a small number of dimensions.

You can be the best by **providing a subset of features that some people would love:**

- Budget airlines chose a single dimension in which to excel: **low headline prices.** They lowered headline prices by cutting costs and turning many features into optional upsells, capturing the (large) segment of the market that made its decision based primarily on headline price.
- Our client daFlores is an e-commerce store that became successful by delivering a **restricted range of products**—flowers—to a **restricted geographical location**—Latin America—at a time when its competitors hadn't established the infrastructure to provide this service.

Often, you can niche by **targeting a particular group of customers.** For example,

- Our client Voices.com is a job site that serves only **voice-over artists and people who are seeking voice-over artists.**
- Our client Moz serves **SEOs.** Moz's product has changed over the years, but its target market has remained roughly the same throughout.

Niching often wins

When you niche your service to a particular group of needs or customers, you get several powerful advantages. To illustrate the point, consider shampoo. If you study the shelves of a supermarket, you'll see shampoo for the following:

- Oily, itchy, and greasy hair
- Heavily dandruffy hair
- Suave professional hair
- Hair with fox poo it (to be fair, this one may not be in the same section of the supermarket)

In fact, you'd struggle to find general-purpose shampoo that isn't niched to a particular type of hair.

Niched shampoos have displaced all the non-niched ones, because they have been more successful with customers.

Four reasons why niching usually wins

Do you need help with any of the following?

Basic oboe or recorder lessons

Cleaning

Logo Design

Babysitting

Gardening

Event & product photography

and other odd jobs...

Contact me:

on

An un-niched service (though clearly a multitalented person).

Niching is effective for several reasons:

1. **A niched product is worded in terms of the cus-**

tomer's need. The niched product effectively says, "I understand your situation, and I am a ready-made solution for it." **It's hard to overlook a product that has been designed to satisfy your exact need.**

2. **People are aware that niched things are often better.** A surgeon who specializes in a rare type of gastric operation will tend to be better at it than a surgeon who hasn't. Specialists tend to be more proficient than generalists, because they have focused their resources on solving a narrower problem. As a result, **most people recognize that specialization is an indicator of high performance.** So even if all shampoo bottles were to contain the same ingredients, customers would still expect the specialist ones to be better.

3. **Niching allows you to become the best in the world.** No one checks into a hotel and asks the concierge, "What's the second-best Chinese restaurant nearby?" Seth Godin argues that buyers always want the best in the world. Though he admits that "the best" depends on what the target segment wants (e.g., Chinese food), and that "the world" may be restricted (e.g., to restaurants within a certain distance of the hotel). Godin argues that, to be successful, a person or company must define the "world" it will be best in, and what it means by "best." And then, crucially, to not fall short.

4. **Things that are niched get attention.** All death-metal bands have similar logos. Except for the band "Party Cannon." See if you can spot Party Cannon's logo:

Going to a death-metal festival? See if you can spot Party Cannon's logo. (Image credit: Party Cannon.)

"Each time our logo goes viral, we gain fans—which is awesome." —Chris, Party Cannon

Niching works best for marginal outsiders

Niching works best in marketplaces that are noisy and overcrowded. By being distinctive, you win a disproportionate amount of attention.

Once you have grown to saturate your niche, though, you need to satisfy more people and needs. At that point, the winning strategy is to become less niched and more moderate.

You see this happen during TV talent shows and political campaigns. At the start of a political campaign, a candidate benefits from being extreme. As the campaign progresses, and competitors are eliminated, the wise candidate mellows, sacrificing attention-getting antics in order to appeal to a broader audience.

Tread on as few toes as possible

The software company HubSpot refuses to offer consulting services. Instead, it operates a partner program for agencies. As a result, many consultancies around the world evangelize HubSpot. If HubSpot had chosen to offer consultancy services, those same companies would have actively avoided recommending HubSpot.

By being niched and focused, your company can be symbiotic with other businesses. Neighboring companies become allies.

By being unfocused and broad, your company treads on more toes. Those allies become competitors.

Exercise restraint when widening the scope of your services. Try to minimize your number of competitors. Keep your footprint small.

How to spot good niches: Three easy techniques you can use

- **Look back at the success you have had over the past year.** You may find that it has a theme. You may have already started niching inadvertently. Amplify that niching by communicating it to your visitors. In his book *Entrepreneurship and Innovation*, Peter Drucker describes how Macy's department store initially downplayed the growing effect of appliance sales on its profits. It considered the sales to be an "embarrassing success." Macy's profits rose only once it embraced appliance sales as a part of its image.
- **As markets grow, they fragment.** If you can pick the next dimension along which your market will fragment, you can get there first. Match.com used to be the only dating website anyone had heard of. As the industry grew, many niched dating sites became successful. There are now successful dating sites aimed at
  - long-term relationships (eHarmony);
  - time-starved professionals (Lovestruck);
  - people who don't want to pay (PlentyOfFish);
  - people of certain religions (ChristianMingle);
  - country folk (Muddy Matches);
  - and, ahem, Tinder.
- **What is luxury today will be mainstream tomorrow.** Study your most advanced, sophisticated, wealthiest users. The problems they have today—and the solutions

they use—will soon be mass market. Such users give you a glimpse of the future. When plasma TVs first came out, they were used only by exhibitors at trade shows. As prices fell, plasma TVs began to be bought by public venues like bars. It took years before they began to be bought for domestic use. What are your sophisticated users buying today? How can you help to make that service mainstream?

Niching works best when you create a new category

When we started working with Mobal, it rented phones to international travelers. So did its competitors. We created a new value proposition for Mobal: a travel-phone you could own for just $49, with no monthly fees.

Suddenly, Mobal was no longer one of many phone-rental companies; it was the $49-travel-phone company. Reviews in travel magazines would say, "If you need a phone when you're abroad, you have two options: (1) rent one or (2) buy a Mobal phone."

By creating a new category, Mobal became 50% of the available options. And gained free coverage in *TIME*, *Inc.*, *Wall Street Journal*, *Washington Post*, and almost every travel magazine.

Six ways to spot niching opportunities your competitors will ignore

One of the most common mistakes is simply to identify an opportunity, and then aim to capture it. Just because something is an opportunity today doesn't mean it's worth chasing.

Instead, **look for opportunities that you can seize without a struggle,** because your competitors won't stop you.

List your opportunities, and then run them through the following checklist, to identify which of them your competitors are likely to avoid:

1. Some competitors will avoid an opportunity because **it runs against their strategy, their brand, and what they stand for:** If Rolex were to start making cars, you could predict with reasonable confidence that it would target the luxury end of the market. Rolex would be unlikely to compete with a company that sells low-end cars. If Ikea were to launch a car, on the other hand, you might expect it to be lower priced and more functionally designed. And maybe you'd need to assemble the engine yourself. Ikea would, therefore, be less likely to compete with a company that sells luxury cars.

2. Coca-Cola brands itself as being an age-old classic. Pepsi is therefore safe to position itself as being modern, because Coca-Cola will not attempt to occupy that position.

3. Some competitors will avoid an opportunity because **it would disrupt their existing business**: When Google first made its office software free, it was safe to assume that Microsoft wouldn't do the same. Such a move would have undermined too much of Microsoft's revenue. In his book *The Innovator's Dilemma*, Clayton Christensen calls this principle *dependency*. Companies depend on their existing customers, revenue, and investors and are unlikely to upset them.

4. You ideally want to focus on an opportunity that will inevitably grow—to "skate where the puck is going." Fortunately, many competitors will avoid such an opportunity because **it isn't big enough yet.** This leaves a gap that you can fill. Even when an opportunity will imminently become large, many competitors will ignore it until it happens.

5. Some competitors will avoid an opportunity because **they have a track record of failing at that activity.** Or not even trying. If a company has always failed at something, or has always avoided doing it, you can predict with reasonable confidence that it will continue to do the same. Often, you'll never find out the reasons. Fortunately, you don't need to. For example, when Yahoo! acquires a tech company, you can be reasonably confident that that tech company will no longer be a threat.

6. Some competitors will avoid an opportunity because **it doesn't match their strengths.** In this respect, it's

helpful to consider what Guy Kawasaki calls "your unfair advantages."

7. Some competitors will avoid an opportunity because **they don't know something that you do.** Your experience may reveal an opportunity that other companies wouldn't even recognize or appreciate.

Are the following psychological biases stopping you from niching?

If niching is so effective, why do so few companies do it? Because niching means overcoming three types of psychological discomfort:

Discomfort 1: Focus = Neglect

Many people agree that they need to focus more. But they think that *focus* means *concentrate*. It doesn't. *Focus* means *neglect*. As Steve Jobs said, "Focus means saying no to the hundred other good ideas." Focusing doesn't feel empowering; it feels embarrassing, upsetting, and scary. **A sign that you are focusing is that you frequently cringe at the things you *aren't* doing.** Your head knows you are doing the right thing, but your stomach turns at the things you are neglecting.

How can you overcome the cringing feeling? Remind yourself that your neglect can be temporary. Once you dominate a particular niche, you can incrementally expand the scope of your business. As Amazon has done. Amazon started by being a bookstore and is heading toward being an everything store.

Discomfort 2: You must ignore social proof

If you see people running out of a building, you would be wise to copy them; maybe the building is on fire. People trust social proof because it's often a reliable indicator. However, it can work against you. **Next time your market research reveals an opportunity and you wonder why no one else has tried it, be aware that your desire for social proof might be the only thing standing between you and success.**

Discomfort 3: You mustn't conform

We tend to behave like those around us, to be liked or accepted. This same instinct can cause marketers to feel a twinge of discomfort every time they stray from the norm. But niching means doing things that others don't. **So next time you feel a twinge of awkwardness because your company is doing something eccentric—because you are sticking your neck out—remind yourself that your desire for conformity might be holding you back.**

The riches in niches

The best way to "beat your competitors" is often to redefine yourself so that you have fewer of them.

Be prepared to go to war, but choose your battles wisely.

Winning websites...keep attention: if your visitors are forgetting about you, here's how to make them keep coming back

Your visitors' browsing sessions get can sidetracked by real life. This family, for example, could possibly get distracted by eating, parenting, or the inevitable breakdown of their relationships.

Your visitors aren't all sitting in a usability testing lab in isolation. They are real people living real lives:

- Their kids might ask to be fed, and they have to abandon their online shopping to go and "cook" a bowl of breakfast cereal.
- Their taxi driver might arrive to take them to line dancing.
- Their dog might knock a glass of red wine onto the floor, and so they hurriedly abandon the life insurance

form they were completing, and instead spend the next twenty minutes mopping an excellently clingy shiraz with apricot top notes out of their rug.

Stuff like that. Real lives can be distracting.

Once your visitors are distracted, they may never come back. How can you, as a web marketer, overcome those problems? You can't make breakfasts. You can't postpone line dancing. You can't absorb wine. So how can you make those visitors come back?

Solution 1: Be memorable enough so that they return

There are many ways to be memorable. Here are just three examples:

- **Have a memorable name:** Once someone has heard the name SurveyMonkey, they are likely to remember it. That's a conversion benefit that many of SurveyMonkey's competitors—Typeform, for example—don't have. If you want to create a great, memorable name for your product or company, we highly recommend you get the book "Hello, My Name is Awesome" by Alexandra Watkins. Alexandra's company, Eat My Words, also offers a useful free PDF.
- **Have an entertaining message:** Dollar Shave Club became famous overnight with a video ad that went viral. Within four years, it sold to Unilever for $1 billion.

- **Be different:** LingsCars is a real business. It's much larger than it appears. It achieves memorability by looking absolutely crazy.

Dollar Shave Club became successful off the back of its entertaining explainer video.

You probably wouldn't want to replicate it, but LingsCars shows how successful a company can be just by standing out.

Solution 2: Establish ways to communicate with the visitors on an ongoing basis

If you can get your visitors' contact details, or get them to follow you, then the pressure's off. You no longer need to persuade them in a single session; you can do it over a period of days, weeks, months, or years.

- **Offer a no-brainer deal with a tiny commitment.** Consider how you could greatly increase the conversion rate of the first visit by greatly reducing the commitment your visitors need to make. We described this in detail in "Step 2: Should you use long or short copy?"

- Persuade your visitors to **follow you** on Facebook, LinkedIn, Twitter, YouTube, or whichever social network is used most in your industry.
- Use **ad retargeting** to persuade your visitors to come back. Retargeted ads are particularly effective. Visitors who visited once tend to be extremely likely to visit again.
- **Collect your visitors' contact details**—their email addresses, postal addresses, and/or phone numbers—and then create a follow-up flow that keeps their attention and persuades them to proceed. In many industries—such as education—this beats everything else.

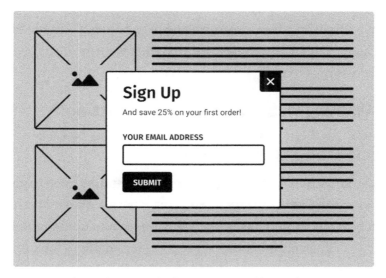

Many companies ask for contact details as soon as the visitors arrive. It may seem a bit "forward" but it works.

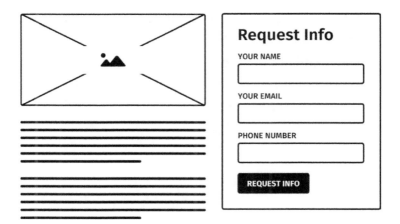

The university-degrees niche is highly competitive. The winning call to action tends to be to collect contact details and then follow up via email and phone.

All of the techniques listed here are effective at turning the relationship into more than a one-night stand.

By using them, your business becomes resilient to hungry kids, taxis, wine stains, and whatever else life throws at your visitors.

Winning websites...get prompt action: if your visitors are taking their time, here's how to get them to act immediately

In exit surveys, visitors often report that they need to go away and think about it. Such responses are particularly common for purchases that are complex and nonurgent.

In such cases, the best solution is usually to look for reasons for urgency.

How travel agents use urgency

The travel industry is masterful at finding reasons for urgency and scarcity—which it expresses frequently throughout booking processes. At every step, there is a genuine reason for the visitor to hurry up.

Let's look for a hotel in New York and see the techniques in action:

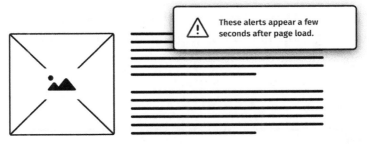

These alerts appear a few seconds after page load.

Notifications often appear over the page a few seconds after it loads, capturing the visitors' attention.

Within seconds of the page loading, a first notification appears in the top-right corner:

There are 14 people looking at this hotel.

Another urgency notification.

Ah, so it's a competition! This communicates scarcity and urgency. Almost immediately, a second notification appears:

This property was booked just 16 minutes ago from the United Kingdom.

An urgency notification.

So those fourteen people aren't just looking; they're booking. Note how the specific details make the urgency more palpable.

A third notification appears:

> **New York City prices for your dates have gone up in the last few hours.**

Another urgency notification.

So not only are rooms selling out, they are becoming more expensive!

And then:

> **Book now! You don't need to pay till you get there. Cancellation is free.**

A notification to communicate low commitment and to reduce the perceived risk.

which lowers the perceived risk of acting urgently.

A minute ago, we were idly browsing hotels. We didn't even know there was a Novotel hotel on Times Square. Now we are caught in a Black Friday-style stampede for it.

Notice how the page elements above don't just repeat

the same message. They manage to express urgency in many subtly different ways.

Framing gains as losses

Ticket brokers focus on urgency too. Imagine you receive an email announcing that an '80s soft metal band are having a reunion tour. You click on it out of curiosity. Before you know it, the ticket broker has reserved particular seats for you, and then show a timer at the side of the page:

A timer on a checkout page adds urgency—particularly when it's getting close to zero.

It's the only animated part of the page, so it flickers its message of urgency in the corner of your eye as you study the page.

This alert doesn't just express urgency. It has turned the decision into a fear of loss. The seat numbers have already been reserved for you; now you just need to decide whether to abandon them or not. According to Prospect Theory, changes that are framed as losses are weighed much more heavily than changes that are framed as gains.

And before you can say "soft-rock poodle perm," you

have bought tickets to see 90 minutes of new romantic power ballads.

How some companies build scarcity into their offers

In our experience, almost all businesses have genuine scarcity and urgency.

However, many companies manufacture scarcity and urgency, in the same way that they manufacture their products. Manufacturers of luxury goods, like Rolex, Ferrari, Louis Vuitton, build scarcity into their marketing plans.

Even if the product isn't scarce, the offer can be. Companies like Bose create rolling time-limited offers. For example, Bose might offer free accessories for anyone who orders by the end of the month. But what happens the following month? No more offer? Instead, the offer simply switches to another time-limited offer, which expires at the end of that month. Such offers allow the company to always have a reason for the visitor to act promptly. An extreme example of rolling time-limited offers are daily deals websites.

Principles of urgency

Urgency is about time. Explore reasons why your visitors should act promptly.

- Whenever possible, **have a deadline**, and always give a reason why the deadline exists.

- If there are no inevitable deadlines, consider creating deadlines. For example, offer a premium or discount for people who respond within a certain period. (For example, conferences usually have an early bird registration period.)
- **Look for scarcity** in your business. Scarcity causes an inevitable deadline—the time at which the scarce resource runs out.

Winning websites...thrive in an imperfect world: if parts of your sales funnel are outside of your control (and are terrible), here's how to win regardless

Are parts of your sales funnel outside of your control?

Many marketers have their hands tied, unable to edit crucial parts of their funnels.

This is particularly common for businesses that are paid for generating leads for other businesses—for example, for financial services, education, health care, or real estate:

- **A financial services company** might send its visitors to an application form on a bank's website. If the bank's website is terrible (many are), what can the financial services company do?
- **A college education broker** might send its leads to an

application form on a particular college's website. If the college's website is terrible (many are), what can the broker do?

- **A real estate broker or a health care provider** might send its visitors to a local sales team that is terrible at closing the deal (many are). What can the real estate broker do?

The problem also occurs when part of the funnel is managed by a different department that isn't interested in doing CRO. This happens surprisingly often. For example, many of our clients hire us for help with their marketing materials, but then discover through our research that numerous opportunities lie within the onboarding and usability of the product itself. This is really common with web app companies.

The "other" part of the organization is typically much worse at CRO. (We presume it's because of the Dunning-Kruger effect; people who lack particular skills also lack the metacognition to appreciate their lack of skills.)

Regardless, it's frustrating—for your visitors, who have to face the Handover of Death, and for you, who knows it could be prevented.

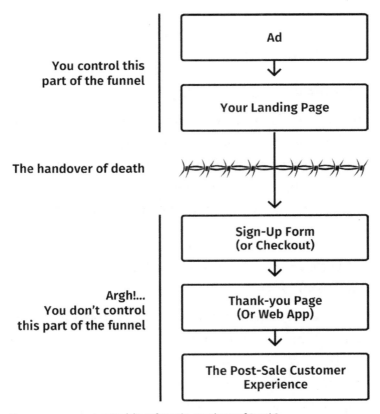

How can you protect your visitors from the Handover of Death?

Seven effective remedies for when you don't control the conversion page

Here's what you can do to fix the problem:

1. Ensure your visitors are fully persuaded

Ensure that your visitors are fully persuaded before they leave your website. **Don't rush them to leave.** Don't push them into a checkout process, for example, before they are persuaded to take action.

2. Ensure your visitors qualify

Before your visitors leave, ensure that they *qualify* for the product they are considering. Financial products, for example, often have many qualification criteria. If you send a visitor to apply for a mortgage that they aren't qualified for, they won't (can't) convert, and you are unlikely to see them again.

3. Hustle your tracking code onto the ultimate conversion page

If you are only able to track when someone clicks away from your website, you will optimize your business for click-outs, not for conversions. So do whatever you can to put tracking code on the ultimate conversion page—even if it takes some negotiating and hustling. That way, you can optimize for the true goal.

4. Be a destination, not just the station

Build a relationship with your visitors. You don't want to simply be the station that your visitors pass through on the way to their final destination. Find ways of providing value to them, so they come to see you as a trusted advisor. Get their contact details, or get them to follow you on social media, so they remember to return next time they need your advice.

5. Be memorable

Be memorable in terms of your name and branding, **so that visitors think of you next time they have the same need.**

6. Have a reason why visitors should order via you

Offer visitors a reason to order via you rather than via a competitor. A highly effective technique is to give away information, because the marginal cost of doing so is almost zero, yet it can provide significant value to the customer. Information can be a deal maker. Shell Oil did this with outrageous success by giving away booklets about motoring. The booklets had titles like "How you can spot some car problems before they cost big money" and "How to save gasoline when you buy a car, drive a car, and take care of a car." The campaign was reported to be Shell's most success-ful ever, with three hundred million booklets given away.

7. Expand your influence

Do whatever you can to **get permission to edit those parts of the funnel that aren't in your control.** One of our clients, a phone company, discovered that one-third of all its inbound calls were from customers inquiring how to use the travel adapters that came free with the phones. We decided to contact the company that made the travel adapters and offered to redesign its packaging to make it more usable. After several rounds of iteratively designing and then usability testing, we sent off the much-improved packaging designs to the manufacturer. Several weeks later, when customers started receiving the newly designed travel adapters, the problematic inbound customer calls dropped to zero.

Winning websites...have a huge lifetime customer value (LCV): how to identify opportunities to increase your LCV, the powerful conversion metric that people forget about

Some people wrongly believe that CRO stops when a customer places an order. In fact, increasing repeat purchases is one of the easiest way to grow your business. Another is to enthuse customers to tell their friends. In this chapter, you'll learn some techniques to turn visitors into raving fans who love your company, spend a lot, and tell their friends to do the same.

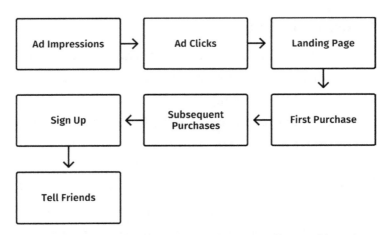

Your conversion funnel extends to the whole customer experience—and beyond.

To win at conversion, you must win at LCV. The most successful companies can outbid their competitors in advertising—not just because they *outconvert* their competitors, but also because their customers *keep returning to spend more*. That way, the cost of acquiring a customer can be recouped over the total lifetime of the customer.

Furthermore, existing customers are easier to convert—provided they had a good experience first time round.

So how can you get customers to spend more, and more often? We have worked with many companies, and we have noticed commonalities in the ones that have become most successful. The following sections reveal our observations on what works.

A mindset to maximize LCV

Does success come to those who deserve it?

Until recently, the answer was no. But the world is changing quickly, and the answer is moving toward yes. Good people—and good companies—are increasingly getting what they deserve. The phrase "If you build it, they will come" used to be a "falsism." But the internet has made consumers much better at finding great products and services.

Here's an example. In the past, a bad restaurant in a tourist hotspot could prosper by preying on an endless supply of naive customers. Now, thanks to sites like TripAdvisor, prospective diners can find out the truth. So diners go to the best restaurants and they avoid the bad ones. The top-rated restaurants get almost all of the money.

If we ran a restaurant, we'd focus on delivering value—by cooking great food and making customers happy—in the firm belief that everything else would look after itself, because the truth would get out.

If your core value isn't high, you'll get almost no rewards until you become the best available option for your target market—at which point the rewards come rushing in. Because everyone wants the best. No one goes shopping for their second-best option.

So if you were running a restaurant, you'd want your food and service to be not just good but the best, and you'd want your employees to be not just happy but the happiest, because being best is disproportionately more fruitful than being second, third, or fourth. (Of course, the definition of best requires you to niche to a particular target market and a particular offering; a fast-food restaurant is the best at satisfying particular needs of particular customers.)

So we advise our clients to "become deserving of what you want." To build a company that deserves to be hugely successful, because it's the best in the world at delivering value. To focus their efforts on delivering and improving every aspect of their service.

This isn't just nice-to-hear fluff. Many marketers are attracted to short-term hacks and black-hat secrets. (If you ever go to a conference where one of the talks has a title that mentions sneaky tricks, notice how full the room is.)

We find those that win at conversion tend to be those that aim to build something great.

Use Net Promoter Score to improve customer happiness

How can you measure whether you're turning visitors into raving fans? *Net Promoter Score (NPS)* can be simple and effective. To measure your raving-fan-ness, simply ask your customers the following question: "On a scale of 0 to 10, how likely are you to recommend us to a friend or colleague?" You then calculate the percentage of respondents who gave scores of 9 or 10 (NPS calls those people "Promoters"), and then subtract the percentage of respondents who gave scores of 0 to 6 (NPS calls them "Detractors"). The theory is that Promoters will grow your business via word of mouth and that Detractors will shrink your business via word of mouth. An NPS of +100 would mean that every customer would be a raving fan, evangelizing you wherever they go. An NPS of –100 would mean the opposite, that every customer is out there complaining. NPS isn't just useful as a metric; it's useful as a concept. An NPS of +100 is a guiding star that every team member can envisage and strive for.

Your raving fans are likely to make subsequent purchases, and they are likely to recommend you to their friends.

Upsell and cross-sell

In addition to selling more of the same thing, you can also increase LCV by satisfying additional needs. In the chapter about giving people what they want, we described a process to identify what your customers will buy from you, and how to explore which of those opportunities will make the biggest impact.

No bounds: Let CRO permeate every aspect of a business

One of our clients sells sheds online. Our CEO, Ben, was the most in need of a new shed. (More accurately, he was the person *least reluctant* to get one.) Ben had many insights during the buying process. One of the more interesting insights came once the shed was delivered to the front of his house. Ben discovered that the shed's components would not fit easily through a standard doorway. They scraped the paint off the house's door frame. Based on this feedback, our client redesigned all its sheds so that no component was too large to fit through a doorway. This improved the client's customer feedback rating, which was already high.

In buying and constructing this shed, Ben made an observation that led to the manufacturer redesigning its entire range.

Some people would deem shed-testing to be outside of the remit of CRO. You can apply your CRO skills to every aspect of a business, throughout the whole customer experience. We've applied CRO to offline advertising, explainer videos, product design, sales scripts, recruitment funnels, training programs—and almost every other aspect of a business.

The following activities are often effective at increasing customer satisfaction and LCV:

- Building the relationship with visitors via regular follow-up—with an email autoresponder sequence or lead-generation welcome pack.

- Being more than a store. Becoming a community and/or a trusted advisor.
- Creating and optimizing a refer-a-friend program.
- Cross-selling on your thank-you page. This can increase the net profit considerably, because you have already acquired the customers, so the additional gross profit goes straight to the bottom line.

See the power of CRO in action

A case study showing exactly how we grew a company at record-breaking speed

A useful case study in conversion: how we helped grow a company by 470% in a year

We helped goHenry to grow by 470% in one year.

It can help to see how a project flows from start to finish. In this section, we describe a project that helped a client of ours to grow by 470%.

In early 2015, goHenry hired us to increase the effectiveness of its digital marketing and grow its market share. goHenry is a financial-technology (FinTech) company that combines web and mobile apps to create a unique learning tool for children. It ranked in the FinTech 100, a list of the top companies in FinTech.

This section describes some of the things we've done. Note that *we* refers to a team effort between Conversion Rate Experts (with our expertise and proven system) and goHenry (with its highly effective team).

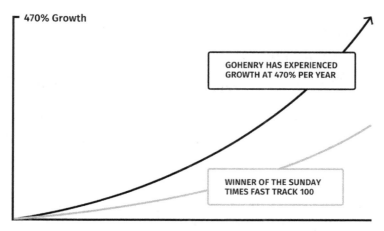

goHenry's growth was faster than the winner of the *Sunday Times* Fast Track 100.

Identifying the biggest opportunity, and adopting a mobile-led approach to optimization

goHenry brought us in because it recognized that there was an opportunity to adopt a faster-moving, more experimental culture.

When we start working with new clients, we look for the big opportunities, **the changes we can put in place quickly that will have a lasting—and scalable—effect on the business.**

We used the following techniques to help identify the opportunities for goHenry:

- **We studied its analytics data to understand existing traffic sources**—which channels were converting best, and where were the big opportunities for growth.

- We had a **session with the goHenry team to discuss its current approach to making changes on the website.**
- We mapped the different aspects of the company's business model, to **identify its "winning business model."**
- We took time to **understand the regulatory regime in which goHenry operates** (which can be particularly onerous for FinTech companies).

Two of the conclusions from the research were especially interesting:

- The winning business model for goHenry required it to grow incredibly quickly—a strategy that we've applied successfully with many of our clients. Businesses like this tend to be "winner takes all." goHenry had the first-mover advantage, which can be formidable provided the pace is kept up. So goHenry would need an approach to optimization that was lean and structured.
- The success of goHenry depended on mobile users, so we'd need to build the workflow around mobile from the get-go.

Stepping into the visitors' shoes—and why you should focus on mobile in isolation

Before we made any changes on the website, **we listened to what the visitors were telling us.** Because goHenry's visitors were on mobile devices, **we listened to what the** *mobile* **visitors were telling us.** It sounds obvious, but it's often overlooked—even by companies with sophisticated mobile websites.

Don't assume that your mobile visitors are just desktop visitors on a different device. If you do, you'll focus on the user interface as the only difference between the two.

In fact—as we discovered when we gathered data on goHenry's visitors—mobile users can have very different intentions, likes, and objections to their desktop counterparts. You'll need to address these specifically on your mobile journey.

Some things we learned about goHenry's mobile visitors (and how they're different from desktop visitors)

The difference between mobile users and desktop users isn't just about screen size. Mobile users are more likely to have arrived from a social network, so they were different in the following respects:

1. **Mobile users were more impulsive.** Many landed on the site on a whim—so knew much less about what was being offered. That's bad news when you're selling a new and innovative product, like goHenry.
2. **They were 50% less likely to have their children with them when they signed up.** Remember, goHenry is a product for children, so this affected the mechanics of the new funnel as well as the messaging we used.

3. **They were 40% more likely to have concerns about trust and security** (which are tough objections for a FinTech to overcome).

Gather and analyze data on your mobile visitors in isolation—otherwise valuable insights could be lost in the noise.

Knee-deep in insights about goHenry's mobile visitors, we set about designing a new mobile conversion funnel.

Here's what happened.

A new mobile landing page increased sign-ups by 78%

Using our insights on mobile visitors—and our workflow for developing high-converting pages for them—we created a new landing page for goHenry.

It won an A/B test convincingly, increasing sign-ups by 78% over the original. Here it is:

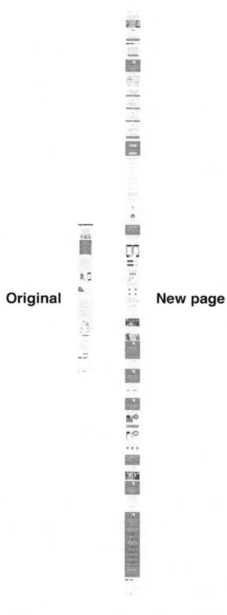

Original   **New page**

At 2.5 m tall on mobile, our new page may have problems getting through doorways, but it had no problem beating the original page by 78%.

There are loads of reasons why our new page beat the original. Here are just some of the proven techniques we used:

Reasons it won #1: We had a long story to tell, so we created a long page

Our mobile visitors were intrigued but had many strong objections—as you would expect when selling a new financial product for children.

A long page allows us to address systematically all of the key objections, starting with the strongest.

Then, as each objection was addressed, we gave the prospect an opportunity to proceed through the funnel by sprinkling the "call to action" throughout the page. This effectively made the page as short as possible—but as long as necessary. This was particularly important on mobile.

There's no such thing as a too-long page—only a too-boring one. So we had to ensure that the page was engaging from top to bottom.

Reasons it won #2: We used visual ways to present the information

Our research revealed that mobile visitors landed on the website with only a vague idea of what was being offered. Coupled with their strong objections, we were dealing with seriously volatile visitors, liable to self-destruct (leave the website) at any time.

We had to find ways to get our message across quickly.

Just some of the ways we used to communicate the offer on mobile (all taken from the same page).

Notice that the previous techniques use visual methods for presenting complex information. Done right, this can be especially effective on mobile, where attention spans are as small as the screens.

Reasons it won #3: We built trust and credibility—fast

Selling a new financial product and selling a new product for children are two of the toughest gigs in town. Buyers understandably have issues with trust and credibility.

Combining the two—selling a new financial product *for* children—is particularly difficult.

This became obvious when we looked at our research data.

By using the trust inherent in the Visa brand, we wiped out issues with trust and credibility.

We needed something that would wipe out trust issues fast.

The answer lay in the fact that goHenry is backed by Visa, one of the world's most well-known and trusted financial institutions.

By positioning Visa much more prominently as part of the proposition—showing it even more prominently than the goHenry brand—we reassured visitors that goHenry was associated with a brand they already trusted.

Do you have similar examples of "hidden wealth" in your business? Most of our clients have elements that could be highly persuasive to prospects, but that the prospects rarely see. Used correctly, such persuasion assets can be amazingly effective. It's worth thoroughly searching your own business. Often, a fresh pair of eyes will spot something you've overlooked.

We created a 191% increase from optimizing mobile Facebook ads

When you've gathered loads of insights on your visitors, it's crazy to focus only on the website. **Every interaction a prospect, visitor, or customer has with your business is an opportunity for optimization.** Constantly look for other areas to apply your learnings. We use our research across all areas of the business, including offline.

Facebook was goHenry's primary source of acquisition, so it was an obvious candidate for us to work on. We optimized goHenry's Facebook ad campaign, applying multivariate testing to its ad creatives. By sending the ads to our winning landing pages, **we increased the number of sign-ups by 191% (that's nearly three times).**

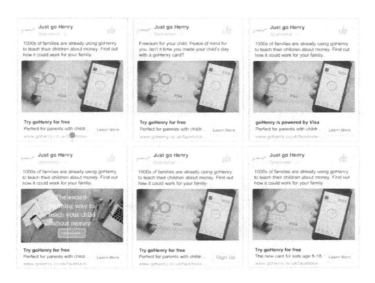

So far, we've multivariate tested over 100 Facebook ads.

We created a 36% increase in sign-ups from optimizing the pricing page

We knew that price was a major pain point for prospects, so we turned our attention to the pricing page. Also, prospects had objections about being locked in and how to cancel the subscription.

We designed a new page to address these issues. **It increased sign-ups by 36% over the original:**

Original

New page

During the A/B test, our new pricing page beat the control by 36%. You'll see that it includes more salesmanship than the original. Many companies make the mistake of assuming that they don't need to do any selling on their pricing page.

Here are some of the ways we addressed the pricing and trust objections:

Try the Award-Winning Online Learning Tool for Children— completely FREE for 3 months

Thousands of parents are discovering why goHenry is an easy (and fun) way to pay pocket money and teach your kids about money.

In the absence of obvious competitors to goHenry, prospects were using bank accounts as their "frame of reference." But bank accounts are free. We communicated that goHenry is much more than a payment account—it's an online learning tool. As such, its price is extremely low.

That's why, for a limited time, we are offering a completely FREE one month trial

After 1 month—**ONLY if you're 100% delighted with goHenry**—you can choose to move onto our paid plan for just £2.49 per child per month

Try goHenry for **free**

Pricing objections peaked on the pricing page, so we added our primary counterobjection: the free trial.

Plus, you'll never pay a penny for these great services:

- Free UK cash withdrawals.
- No overdrafts, so no overdraft fees.
- Free goHenry card for your child to use.
- Free telephone and email support, so you'll always have help when you need it.
- Load your accout for free using Standing Order or bank transfer.

On the pricing page, don't forget to remind prospects of the value of your product. We added a section covering all the great free features bundled with goHenry and an image showing how much "stuff" you get.

We created a 23% increase in sign-ups from homepage optimization

We've already described how our new landing page beat the original by 78%.

Next, we tested it against the current homepage. It won again, by 23%.

It won because our research told us that half of the visitors to the homepage were originally from the same source as those on the landing page—they were just returning for a second look. So it followed that they would have the same objections and be persuaded by the same appeals.

How did we know this? We asked them.

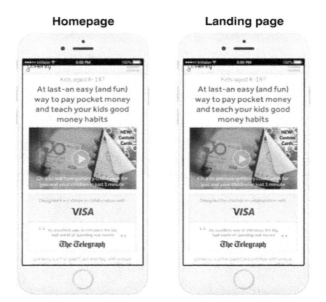

Recycle, recycle, recycle—if you have winning content, look for other places you can use it.

Do you know where your customers come from? If you don't, ask them the following question: "Where did you first hear about us?"

You might be surprised at the answer.

We created an 8% uplift in card activations from optimizing the postsale pages

Having made a huge impact increasing sign-ups, we turned our attention to the activation funnel. When a child's card arrives in the mail, the parent must first activate it before it can be used. This stage is crucial for goHenry; each unactivated card is wasted money.

Before we began optimizing the card-activation stage, we carried out dedicated usability studies. The studies revealed two main issues:

- The activation process began with the standard member log-in screen. Many parents didn't consider themselves members at this point, so weren't sure they were in the right place.
- There were a several "cognitive barriers" on the journey, things that made members stop and think, diverting attention from the task at hand.

When we designed a new funnel to address these issues, card activations increased by 8%.

Original	New page

Signpost your website so that visitors know they're in the right place.

Original	New version

Be ruthless when designing your journeys—focus only on what's necessary to complete the task at hand. When parents were asked to load money into their account, they had to define the amount in terms of a weekly allowance (unnecessary decision #1), and how many weeks' allowance to add (unnecessary decision #2). Our new design removed both of these decisions.

We created an 11% uplift in card activations from optimizing the offline journey

Don't just limit optimization to your website. If part of your journey happens offline, optimize that too.

That's exactly what we did with goHenry's card activation journey.

Our research told us that half of the children knew about the card before it arrived in the mail. Now, if you've got kids you'll know how persuasive they can be, so it came as no surprise that parents were more likely to activate when their child knew about the card.

It followed that if we could make more kids aware of the card, more cards would be activated.

So we sent the welcome letter to the kids instead. After all, the purpose of goHenry is to teach children financial responsibility.

The result? Card activations increased by 11%.

By sending the card and letter to kids (the letter on the right), we increased activations by 11%, as measured using an offline A/B test.

Some of the tools we used on the goHenry project

Here are just a few of them:

- We use Qualaroo or Hotjar to add **mobile-specific pop-up surveys** to key pages.
- **Each interaction between finger and screen expresses an *intent***—and you need to understand what it is. Tools like Hotjar, Crazy Egg, and Inspectlet will help you do just that.
- For maximum insights, **use mobile screen recording software to capture usability tests (or simply record the test on another device).** We use Lookback to build an army of usability testers—or test recruiters—and have the videos land right in your inbox. It will even film the subject's face during the test.

- If you can't get friends or colleagues to help, use sites like UserTesting.com to do remote usability testing on mobile. (**Tip: we love UserTesting.com's webcam-based tests for mobile, so look out for this option.**)
- Use tools like SurveyMonkey to conduct quick straw polls. Verify is a good alternative.
- **Make sure you can quickly view your wireframes on mobile.** We use InVision to rapidly add functionality to our mobile wireframes. Then, we combine the wireframes with screenshots to create a semiworking version of the entire funnel. Finally, we use a service like UserTesting.com to **test the prototype funnel**.
- We use **A/B testing software like Optimizely to measure which page generates the most conversions.** Optimizely's advanced custom audience features came into their own on this project. Tests that would have been prohibitively complex to run were suddenly within reach.

A tip for succeeding in highly regulated industries

If, like goHenry, you're working in financial services—or any tightly regulated vertical—you'll need to work closely with risk and compliance teams. This can be a major bottleneck in getting your ideas approved. Where possible, submit your ideas in "bite-size" chunks, each with a mini-business case. Complexity in these submissions can otherwise be crippling. Such "micro-approvals" are less onerous and much more likely to succeed.

What's next?

We are now working on the goHenry app itself, aiming to drive engagement and referrals.

On the website, we're working on the sign-up funnel, as well as other key parts of the journey such as forgotten password and referrals.

Once complete, we will have rebuilt the entire site.

What's unusual about this rebuild is that it has been done iteratively, and with conversion at the heart of every decision. Conversion, by definition, is the reason that any website exists.

Every new page has been

- driven by visitors and
- measured to make sure it outperforms what went before it.

Nine out of every ten redesign projects we see go wrong. Performance and conversion often nosedive, and expensive—and time-consuming—remedial action is necessary. (We know this because this is why many clients pick up the phone and call us.)

By adopting the iterative approach we have outlined above, we eliminate the risk. Plus, every new page is ROI-positive from the moment it is pushed live.

What about desktop?

We have deliberately ignored desktop in this section, despite the fact that we've worked extensively on goHenry's desktop website. That's because optimizing for mobile is just like optimizing for desktop, but with the following additional obstacles:

- **Mobile users can be more distractible,** because they are often on the move or multitasking.
- **The connection speed** is more likely to be low or intermittent.
- **The keyboard** is more fiddly to use.
- **The screen is much smaller** (and smaller still when the keyboard is active). In particular, users can struggle to complete forms.
- The screen is often being **viewed in bright light,** so low-contrast text and images can be harder to see.

Now it's **your turn to win**

This book contains enough information to hugely grow any business.

More importantly, though, it provides a mental model for improving businesses:

- By understanding your visitors, using the techniques we've mentioned, you'll be able to empathically anticipate what will make them happy.
- And by understanding the key features of winning websites, you'll be identify your own company's obstacles, and then fix them so your company is firing on all cylinders.

We wish you great success in making your website win.

Let's **keep in touch!**

To see the links for all the resources mentioned in this book, visit www.conversion-rate-experts.com/book-links/.

To keep up to date with our new discoveries, you can get our free email newsletter from www.conversion-rate-experts.com/gifts/. When you join, you'll get some useful reports, including examples of winning pages we've designed that have more than doubled the sales of our clients.

We love hearing from readers who have achieved great things by following our ideas and advice, so please let us know how you get on! You can contact us at www.conversion-rate-experts.com/contact-us/.

Acknowledgements

We'd like to thank the following awesome people for helping to create this book:

Dave Redfern, Martin Stone, Jonathan Rozek, Tucker Max, Avinash Kaushik, Ian Claudius, Mark Chait, Adam Costa, Art Crowley, Bradd Libby, Casey Bell, Darcie Connell, Eoin Edwards, Kamil Ropiak, Karol Barzowski, Lotte Larsen, Nicolas Fradet, Nina Bordet, Pawel Banhegyi, Peter Hardingham, Richard Bitz, Vicky Cargill, Will Smith, and Chelsea Batten.

CPSIA information can be obtained
at www.ICGtesting.com
Printed in the USA
BVHW092002270219
541312BV00005BA/9/P